# MILLION POUND MUM
# HOW TO START AN INTERNET BUSINESS

**Hazel Cushion**

**with Mai Davies**

# CONTENTS

Introduction

# Introduction

We all live our lives on the online these days. We shop online, we talk to our friends online, we pay our bills online, we even date online. And if you are reading these words then you are probably among the thousands of women who are thinking of making a living online. Once upon a time you needed bricks and mortar to get a business off the ground, all you need now days is a laptop, a good idea, and gumption.

You may find yourself in the same position as so many other mums, stuck at home with the kids, dreaming of achieving more or making your own money. Or you may have had enough of your job and the daily grind of commuting, pushing and shoving along with everyone else to get to work. Do you dream of a shorter daily commute, one that's only from your bedroom to your kitchen?

People start businesses for all kinds of reasons, but usually the one common theme is that they want to be their own boss, they want to run their own life and not have it run by someone else.

But knowing you want to be your own boss can often be deeply frustrating, because you just don't know what kind of business you could run. You may also have misgivings about whether or not you are capable of running a business. If you are thinking of an internet business, you may feel you don't have the skills. You can use Facebook and Amazon, but running a website? You don't need to be a tech expert, you just need to be armed with the right information and be willing to work hard.

*'We hold ourselves back in ways both big and small, by lacking self-confidence, by pulling back when we should be leaning in.'*

Sheryl Sandberg, Chief Operating Officer, Facebook.No. 6 on Forbes' 'World's 100 Most Powerful Women' List

And you don't have to become an internet giant overnight. You can start small and grow to the size you want. You will have a worldwide audience from your living room. The trick is getting to that audience above the noise of all the other stuff online. But you can do it and you can be very, very successful. It just takes a bit of homework and applying what you learn.

You don't need qualifications, just an appetite to get on. I've met people who run a business empire from a one-page website and PayPal, and others who have enormous and complicated sites with all the whistles and bells you can imagine. The joy of the internet is that it's flexible.

## My Story

Let me tell you my story. I never knew I could run a business and my early years certainly didn't show much promise. As a teenager I was so profoundly depressed that I attempted suicide, then spent the next 6 months in hospital. I went from being the girl doing 12 'O' levels, to leaving school with just two, and a Maths result that was so bad it was ungraded. As you can imagine, my confidence was very low. But things looked up a little when I got a place on a silversmithing course at art college. It wasn't the obvious choice for me, but beating flat sheets of silver into shape proved to be great therapy! So there's a silver lining to every cloud, quite literally in this case.

That course led me to working in Hatton Garden, the jewellery quarter in London, and after a couple of years I landed a job selling Garrard jewellery on the QE2. What an opportunity! I travelled around the world, not once but twice, and gradually worked my way up to being Shop Manager. I realise now that I was full of ideas even then. I won both first and second prize in the company's suggestions competition, and was awarded the grand total of £1,000 – a lot of money back in the 80s!

The nomadic lifestyle of working on board ship set a pattern for the next few years of my life as I continued to be the proverbial rolling stone. I met my husband and we bounced around the world together: living in Florida, France, Bali, and Dubai. We were mostly following his job as he also worked in duty free. There were times when I couldn't work and I found that really frustrating. Like all entrepreneurs, I have to be busy and I have to be achieving something. So I found some charity work to throw myself into, and even helped set up a new charity in Dubai called Gulf for Good.

It may sound quite glamorous, living in different countries, and there were good times, but there were also some really hard ones. While we were living in Bali we tried to start a family. I had always wanted children, but, like so many other women, I struggled with infertility for several years. So in 1996 we turned to IVF and miraculously, after only one attempt, it worked. And boy did it work. Triplets! Felicity, Richard, and Julia. An instant family, three beautiful bundles that all arrived at once. But then I have never been a person who does things by halves.

We were lucky, living in Bali we had lots of help with the triplets and the climate was wonderful. We had two wonderful years bringing up the children, then, just before their second birthday, the Tiger economies collapsed and my husband was made redundant. It was devastating. We went from having an easy, beautiful life to having nothing. Absolutely nothing. We got on a plane without even having any keys in our pockets as we didn't own a house or a car. We had no jobs, no income, and three almost-two-year-olds, and so we had to move in with my mother-in-law for a few months.

Thankfully, my husband soon got another job setting up a beer and wine warehouse in Calais. So it was time to pack our suitcases yet again, and we moved to France. It sounds wonderful, I know, but the weather was cold and bleak and the children were often ill. It was such a shock after living in Bali. Then I came down with glandular fever, and the exhaustion from that made me realise I needed help. My mother decided to come and stay. But she wasn't used to driving in France and drove on the wrong side of the road. She was killed in the lane right outside our house – it was just before the triplets' third birthdays.

As you can imagine, the circumstances of her death made the pain of losing her almost unbearable. I felt we need to get away from that area and so we jumped at the chance when my husband was offered a job in the Middle East. I remember very clearly deciding that this tragedy mustn't affect my children's lives. They were only three and that is such a formative time for children. I'm not religious, but if my mum was ever looking down on me, I wanted her to be proud of how I'd coped.

My mum'd always encouraged me to write and she'd left me some money. I hadn't really listened while she was alive but I used some of the inheritance to sign up for a correspondence writing course. I started to get articles and stories published all around the world and it gave me a real thrill to see my work in print.

But life in Dubai also came to an abrupt end. When the Twin Towers came down in 2001, we decided that it was time for the children and I to leave the Middle East, with my husband staying on to work. So I got the suitcases out again, bundled the children onto a plane, and we came home.

We ended up in West Wales because my mother's best friend had retired there and I knew she'd be a surrogate granny if needed. Apart from her, though, I didn't know a soul, so I joined a writers' group. The group's leader encouraged me to do an MA in Creative Writing at a nearby college, and as I'd already turned forty this seemed an incredible opportunity. They accepted my published work instead of a BA and I started the one-year course. It was the most fun I've ever had with my clothes on! I learnt so much and it was incredibly liberating to let my creative side flow again. On the course, we learnt how to publish a book and I was hooked. I realised being a writer was far too lonely an occupation for me, and so the big bright world of publishing beckoned.

So, you see, I didn't have the best beginning, but I was lucky. When I learned how to publish a book I found something I loved and this is a good place to start when you're looking for a business idea.

Now my business is only partly based on the net, but it's a very important part. Almost 70% of our revenue currently comes from e-books. My customers can download those books from my own websites as well as in other marketplaces. This means that once the book is finished and produced, I don't have to pay for printing, or p&p, I don't need huge storage facilities, and I don't get stuck with books I can't sell. And my customers get what they paid for instantly. It's a win-win. I also use the internet to market my books. My websites are not flashy: www.xcitebooks.co.uk www.accentpress.co.uk. In fact they're downright plain. But they work for me and my business and that's what counts.

## Harvest your History

I think one of the things I found most daunting about setting up a business was the feeling that I wasn't really trained or equipped for it. I remember discussing it with a friend and she laughed and said "But look at all the things you've done – harvest your history and you'll find that's better than any MBA course."

It was great advice and something I use as a bit of an internal mantra – it's a real help when you are feeling a bit all at sea.

What do I mean by this? Well, it's time to rewrite your CV, not adding in extra qualifications (as if we would!) but really looking at every role you've held and realising what it's taught you.

Let's run through mine and you'll start to get the picture.

My first job was as a Saturday girl working in a family jewellers in Guildford. It was a small team, and they were kind and welcoming. They competed with larger chains and cheap jewellery from Argos by providing excellent service, knowing their customers, and getting some stock on appro (this is short for 'on approval') rather than paying up front. If a customer came in wanting a diamond tennis bracelet they could order in some samples for them to choose from without actually committing to buying them. The customer had an excellent selection, enjoyed the occasion of seeing what the owner had found for them, and would almost certainly buy one. The owner had invested his time in getting the bracelets in but he hadn't paid up front for the stock in the hope of a sale. He gained an excellent reputation and really built customer loyalty.

He also had a very clever system for scratching the cost in code on each item – you could only see it using a jewellers' loupe but it meant he instantly knew what he'd paid for an item and how much leeway he had in offering a discount.

**Key Points:** You don't always need to invest in stock to make a sale. Drop shipping, which I explain in Chapter 11, is similar to appro – it allows you to sell an item from a third party to your customer without investing in stock.

Having a system for easily identifying your unit cost can be very important in face-to-face negotiations.

As an art student I worked in McDonald's – I started just at the weekends and evenings but was offered holiday work and eventually a management position. I enjoyed the structure of the company because it made it very easy to progress – if you did what they wanted you quickly got promoted. If you didn't, you stayed right where you were. It was very formulaic and there was no room for personality or creativity but it did offer a very clear career path and rewards system. I'm not sure that they still use the star system – we had yellow name badges and earned stars as we progressed. Admittedly it was a bit of a joke amongst the staff but at the end of the day, most people like their work to be noticed and acknowledged.

**Key Points:** A good training system and career path may be important as your company grows. Meanwhile are there others ways to show your staff that you are noticing and appreciating their work?

My next real learning curve came when I worked on the cruise ships. The shop staff worked six-month contracts and by the end of that time we knew our shops and customers incredibly well. Often the ships were located too far from our Southampton HQ and so we rarely saw the buyers or merchandisers. It seemed to me that at the end of our contracts all our knowledge was just wasted because we'd leave as our replacement arrived and there was no way to pass on what our bestsellers were, what promotions worked best, etc. When the company implemented a suggestion scheme I put forward the idea that departing staff should fill in a simple debrief form and won my thousand pounds for the idea.

**Key Points:** Your staff hold valuable information – make sure you mine it. Encourage your staff to be creative and put forward ideas that will help the company and reward them for it.

My next role at sea was as an emergency relief manager – if turnover was really down, the regular manager was ill, or, as in one case, had run off with all the takings, then I was flown in to take over. The staff were often very demoralised and poorly motivated but I soon discovered that enthusiasm is infectious and money is a great motivator. Often the reason sales were down was just due to very sloppy shopkeeping – the racks in the shops would be full of small size T-shirts and all the others would be in boxes in the store room. Since this was on board American cruise ships there wasn't a huge demand for small sizes! Some staff would kick up at having to strip out the shop and refresh all the stock from the storeroom – until they saw the sales. They were all on commission and we literally doubled the takings in a week.

**Key Points:** The stockroom is a graveyard of opportunities – nothing sells unless it can be seen. We constantly refresh and update our covers to match current trends. Would a new photoshoot for the items on your website make a difference in sales?

Paying a commission does motivate people – affiliate schemes are the modern equivalent for websites. Make sure you have signed up to one so you reward people who send traffic to your site.

Back from sea and newly married, I helped my husband set up a wine business in the south of France. With hindsight we were incredibly naive about starting a business and too used to big corporate budgets. We had some useful skills but made some serious buying errors while we adjusted to the size of our new venture. It can be easy to forget that money is coming directly out of your bank account when you are used to the finance department settling all the invoices. I remember I once bought enough nougat to last five years and it had a shelf life of six months.

**Key Points:** Don't be wooed into thinking you will make more money because the discount is higher for bulk quantities – buy small and see if it sells. Better still, try your idea out first using a drop ship scheme and then you will have real facts upon which to base future purchasing.

I'm afraid our naivety, the 80s recessions, and the fact that we drank any profits meant that the wine business only lasted three years. We left France and moved to Birmingham where I got a job in recruitment. I have always enjoyed sales but this was selling people at a time when there were huge numbers of highly-skilled people out of work – it was a very hard sell. Why would a company pay us several thousand pounds to find them a candidate when, if they advertised, hundreds would apply? Well, that was the reason – they would get swamped and were already under pressure because any slack in the work force had long since been reduced. They simply didn't have the time to sift through all the applicants and arrange all the interviews because they had to be focused on running their businesses in a very difficult climate. They needed a skilled person who could start the job running but they simply couldn't invest the time to find one.

**Key Points:** People will buy services if it means their time can be better spent. To sell the recruitment service we had to demonstrate the time-saving benefits. With sales it is often easy to forget to listen to what your customers' needs are. I remember my boss getting me to sell him the ash tray he'd picked up off his desk. I started talking about it, saying it was made of fine cut glass, durable, strong, and reflected taste and elegance. He stopped me by saying "Sorry, no sale, you're wasting my time. I want ashtrays for my fast food chain which need to be cheap and disposable. Goodbye!"

It was a lesson that I have never forgotten – I should have asked him first what sort of ashtrays he needed, why was he looking for a new supplier, and how many did he usually buy a year. All of these things would have enabled me to pitch and price the right product to him and get the sale.

After that we moved to Bali and I eventually set up my own export company. The markets there are full of amazing handicrafts and very cheap tie-dyed sarongs and clothing. It's a place where you can get things made very easily but there were a lot of people doing exports and a very competitive market. I remember taking a whole load of samples to a cruise ship buyer in the US with high hopes of a big order. I showed her the samples but she didn't seem very interested and said that it wouldn't work because they could never match the prices passengers would see the same item for on shore. "I don't suppose you could put them in a little drawstring bag, could you - something that would also hold their keys, pass, and a lipstick?" I went back and sent her some samples and then we did achieve the order I'd dreamed of.

**Key Points:** Sometimes you just need to repackage an item to make it work. That buyer knew her customers and she knew her competition. The bags cost pence to make but enabled her to charge a higher price and made it a more suitable item for the ship's boutique store. Is there a way you could repackage your services or products to increase their value and desirability?

What has been my biggest lesson since setting up Accent Press? I think I'd have to say the value of PR. We have always punched above our weight in getting good coverage for our books because we try to think like journalists. We pitch them a complete story that will give them newsworthy content, which can be hard – just publishing another book is never newsworthy. The other thing is that you can never be certain of the impact of coverage – Elton John shared a post about one of our books to his Facebook fans which resulted in over 7000 clicks on the link, but only a handful of sales. Yet a diet book we published was mentioned in a single paragraph on page 12 of a Scottish newspaper, and we sold 800 copies.

**Key points:** Be a total media tart – flaunt what you have, whenever you can, but be professional about it. They love well-prepared copy that contains reliable surveys and statistics. Consider signing up for a news service like Response Source to get leads on what journalists are looking for.

### What's in this book?

There are so many things to consider before you start running your own business. Business plans, banking, limited companies, branding, and raising finance. All of that is covered in the first book in this series, *Million Pound Mum*. So if you need to get some more information on business skills or inspiration for your future business, do have a look at that.

In this book we're going to look specifically at what you need to know to get an internet business up and running.

Everyone has different levels of knowledge about the web so in writing this book I am going to assume a few things about you.

I am going to assume that, like many mums …

- You're curious and willing to 'turn every day into a school day'. That is my business mantra for any kind of business and it certainly applies to the net. You must be willing to learn and adapt as technology changes.
- You want to run your own life, even if that means taking some risks.
- You are looking for a way to make money online without a bricks-and-mortar business. (Although if you want to do both then this book still applies to you.)
- You're comfortable using computers, browsing the net, and using e-mail regularly.
- You've done some online shopping and perhaps even sold a few things on eBay or Amazon, even if it was just to get rid of stuff you didn't want.
- You're willing to find out about new technologies.
- You want to use the web and online technologies to build your own brand, whatever that may be.
- You're willing to using social media like Twitter and Facebook to reach potential customers and fans.

If this sounds like you then you probably already realise that the web offers limitless opportunities if you want to grasp them. So let's get on with finding out how.

# Section One

# Deciding to Go Online

## Chapter One
## Why an Internet Business?

First of all let's look at the motivation for setting up online. You may have already decided that's what you want to do or you may be wondering if it's the right way to go.

Well, quite simply, an internet business allows you ...

- To connect to billions of potential customers.
- To connect to those customers 24 hours a day.
- Keep your set-up costs low.
- To do all that from one shop window.

Sounds perfect, doesn't it? Well, don't forget that since it's a great idea, lots of other people are doing it too. Although you can get a business up and running really quickly, your competitors can get going just as fast. You will be entering a marketplace where there is lots of competition unless your product or service is unique, which is rare.

But don't let this put you off. Most of your competition will not be doing the same homework as you and will be blundering around on the net wondering why no one is buying from them. Or they may be so large that they can't respond quickly to customers and provide a more personalised service. If you set up correctly and do your marketing well, you stand a good chance of leaving the competition standing.

One of the big advantages of running an online business is that the tiniest company can compete on pretty much an equal footing with a huge multinational. All your customers know about you is what they see on your site. They don't know if you operate from plush offices with a hundred water coolers and a king-sized board room, or a shed in the back garden. They have no idea of the size of your business. As long as your site is well-designed, runs smoothly, and doesn't mislead customers, you can appear just as smart and efficient as M&S or Next.

And your business can be scaled to suit you and your ambitions. You can run an internet business alongside an existing job. This makes it very attractive to mums who may be nervous about chucking their job and taking a risk. It allows you the option of dipping your toe in the water to see how it goes. It also means that you don't have to employ the staff you might need in a real-world business because so many of the things you'd need people for can be done by software in an online business.

You do need people to come to your site, though. People with real shops in popular areas can sit back and wait for people to wander in. Not so with e-commerce. You have to be pro-active and market your site, you can't rely on passing trade as there's no such thing online.

A website needs traffic (people who visit your website) and it needs conversions (turning the people who visit your website into customers who actually buy something).

It's important to look at your website like a physical shop. You still need to think of having a relationship with your customer, especially *after* they've pressed the 'Buy' button.

Start-up Costs

You don't need to rent a shop unit. Instead of a lease on a premises you will be paying for website hosting instead. You won't need to spend a fortune on shelving and décor, you'll just need a shopping cart. And paying for newspaper, magazine, or TV adverts will be replaced by targeted online ads.

24/7

There'll be no closing for Bank Holidays, sick children, Sunday trading, or family weddings – you can trade all day and all night, and all year round.

But don't be fooled into thinking that the business will run itself once it's set up. This is just the start, but it is a major plus point. Of course, if you sell downloadable products like I do, you can wake up in the morning and find that you've made money while you were asleep. But you still have to do the marketing beforehand, so that people want to come to your site in the dead of night to give you their money!

There's quite a learning curve involved in making your site profitable. But you have probably heard the phrase 'Work *on* your business, not *in* it!' This is especially true online.

My websites may not be flashy but they work for my business; most people buying books prefer to do so from the retailers that produce e-reading devices like Amazon's Kindle. Therefore they are more of a shop window and marketing tool. I spend an enormous amount of effort on marketing and networking because that's what raises our company profile and generates consumer interest, but for most paid ads I link through to retailers' sites rather than our own. At the end of the day, business is all about sales and knowing how and why your customer likes to shop. I know that investing in an incredibly expensive site won't earn a return on investment because I can never beat the Amazon offer or change my customers' buying pattern.

E-commerce can be fun and exciting and you can be part of that 3% who make money in the first three years. But to do that you need to plan, research, and implement the right strategies.

## Chapter Two
## What Type of Internet Business?

I'm sure you are confused about what type of internet business you think you could start. Are you bamboozled by the sheer variety of stuff you come across online on a daily basis? Don't let this panic you into paralysis. There are only three basic ways the internet can help a business:

- Selling goods and services
- Selling information
- Supporting a bricks-and-mortar business

That's it! They all break down in the end into one of those three categories. So you need to start thinking about which category you'd like to belong to. If you're not interested in a real-world business and only want to be online, then there are only two categories you could fit into.

### Selling Goods and Services

Online retailing is the obvious benefit of the internet. If you want to sell clothes in a bricks-and-mortar shop, you need staff, expensive shop-fittings, tills, and stock-management software.

But online, all of the infrastructure from the stock management to the payment processing and product display can be bought at a reasonable price.

If you are selling services, either online or real-world services, then your website is simply your shop window.

### Selling Downloadable Products

Fast broadband has given birth to a whole new category of

products – information products. Because they're not physical, you need hold no stock, so you have no storage problems and you won't get stuck with an expensive mistake if it doesn't sell. I have been stuck with printed books in my company when I made a mistake, and getting it wrong almost crashed my company more than once. So I am a huge fan of downloadable products. It means I can keep a huge range of titles permanently available and it's far better for the trees and environment as we are not shipping and trucking books around the world. Also, if there is a mistake it can be easily rectified: covers can constantly be changed and updateds

to suit current trends, and we can play with pricing in a way you can't with printed books. E-books also offer our customers much better value for money so there really are a great many benefits to this format.

### Selling Information

I am sure you have come across many of the internet marketing gurus who sell their products online. The one thing they all push is information products. They package their knowledge and sell it as a downloadable e-book or a video.

People have made millions selling either information products, selling very small numbers of thousands of different products, or selling one very low cost product millions of times. When you add it all up, it amounts to a very respectable revenue.

One word of caution here: web users are getting more sophisticated. Most of us expect to be able to find information for free online these days. So to sell information you have to convince your potential customers that what you are offering is not available for nothing just a couple of mouse clicks away, or that you have taken the pain out of searching for very specific information. If you are truly an expert in your field and you convince your customers that you can deliver value for money, then you might have a winner.

## Using Google to Find Trends

The internet isn't just a place to start a business, it can be a place to find a business idea. If you are looking to catch a trend then Google is your friend. If you find you are at the beginning of a trend you can make a lot of money. Though if you come in at the tail end, you may find your business is short-lived.

Use Google's trend tool to show you what is trending in searches globally. Go to www.google.com/trends. This shows the volume of searches over a given time so you can see whether there is a growing or declining trend. It will show you where in the world there is most interest in your search terms and will give you related terms and how popular those terms are as search words.

Warning – the peaks and troughs on the graphs are a *percentage* of overall searches. The graphs don't tell you whether the *actual* number of searches has gone up or down. This is a measure of the popularity of your topic.

## Find What People are Hungry For

Not only is it possible to find trends, but Google makes it possible to find out exactly what people are searching for on the net, which gives you a big clue as to what they are willing to pay for.

Google has a keyword tool which lets you find how many searches certain words have. 'Keywords' is the term used for the words people use to search for things. (www.google.com/keyword planner)

So if you entered 'women independent travelling' you might see how many people have searched for that. You can refine your search over and over until you find a niche that might be worth exploiting. Then go and search the web to see who is meeting that need and if you could step in and make a profit.

## Chapter Three
## Big Mistakes

There are so many common e-commerce mistakes that it really is worth devoting a chapter to them. After all, if you know where the elephant traps are, you can avoid them. And I have always believed that you learn in business from mistakes, so what better than learning from other people's mistakes?

### Failure to Plan and Forecast

You know what they say – if you fail to plan, you plan to fail. That's especially true online. You have to find out some crucial pieces of information:

- Is there a demand for your product and is that demand online?
- Are the products or services you want to sell already selling online, and how many are selling?
- What's your potential competition's pricing structure? Are they selling for less than you can afford to sell at?
- Have you worked out if your business can be profitable?

### Waiting Too Long

Now, just because you can get a website up in a day and slam in a PayPal option to take money doesn't mean it's always a good idea to set up in a screaming rush. But you can plan too much. You can paralyse yourself with too much research. It will take time for people to find your website, so it isn't a disaster if the website is live before it's ready because it allows you to test it in the real world environment.

## Bad Design

What your website looks like is the impression your potential customer has of your company. When you go to a new website, how long do you take to decide whether you are going to bother to look around or whether you will click away? About 5–7 seconds? That's how long your potential customers will give you, so design is important. When visitors leave your site it's known as 'bounce', and the 'bounce rate' is the measurement used for the percentage of visitors who only look at one page on your site before leaving.

## Clutter

No one can accuse me of having cluttered websites; they are as bare as it's possible to be. But my customers don't have trouble navigating my sites. How often have you been to a website and been bombarded with images, gimmicks, and options. How quickly do you give up? Quite quickly, I'd imagine – I know I do. I add to that bounce rate pretty sharpish. And if I am trying to buy something and there isn't a clear and quick path to the checkout in very few clicks, then I'm off. Design has to be simple and clear and direct. It should be all about leading your customers easily to the checkout in as few clicks as possible. Under 1 in every 100 visitors to the average site will buy something. If you want to increase this percentage you have to make your site easy and quick to navigate. If they have to think, they're gone!

## Poor Software

If you use poor quality e-commerce software then your potential customer is not going to have an enjoyable time trying to buy from you. It'll load slowly, your products will be displayed badly, it may take too many clicks to get through to the shopping cart, and your customer will give up halfway through.

Get good software that allows Google to index your products easily and your customers to get around your site easily. You also want software that effectively automates laborious tasks and processes so you can get on with marketing.

## Poor Keyword Selection

People search for what they want by entering words into the Google search box. Your site should contain the words that people would use to find your products. These are called 'keywords'. Too many websites don't match those words. When you write the content on your pages, you need to be using those keywords so that Google can find them.

## Bad Content

When you write your content it needs to capture your potential customers' attention. If it's boring or not informative then your customers won't stay. Staying on a site is known as 'sticking'. You want your website to be sticky.

## Failing to Analyse the Data

There is free information on the behaviour of the people who enter your site. You can use your e-commerce admin statistics, your server logs from your hosting account, and Google Analytics. These will tell you where your visitors have been on your site, what they looked at, and how long they spent there. If you don't mine this data you're not going to succeed. It can help you target your marketing and your products far more effectively to turn visitors into customers. You can fix the areas that aren't working or dump them altogether and spend more attention on the bits that are working.

## No Follow-Up

Is it the end once someone has bought from you? Well, it is if you don't want to make a profit. A serious web entrepreneur will know the value of back-end marketing. Once you have a customer, communicate with them, build a relationship with them, fix things quickly if they go wrong, and they will come back and buy again. This repeat custom is what really supercharges a business.

# Section Two

# Building Your Website

## Chapter Four
## Finding the Right Website Designer

Remember that over 90% of e-commerce websites struggle to make a profit in their first three years? Now that's a scary statistic. But you have to remember that they fail because they don't plan properly. So if you do your research and plan correctly you can be part of the 10% that do make money in their first three years.

The planning starts with your design. I am assuming you have no desire to learn how to code and build your site from scratch. So let's have a look at web designers you might hire. When I say 'designers', I mean any company that will build your site. I'll cover building a website yourself at the end of the chapter.

Most of the companies out there have never sold online themselves. So you need to find a company that really understands what you need.

You should make sure you are in regular communication with your design team to ensure they are doing what you want and not wandering off in another direction.

### Getting Quotes

In order to get a quote for designing your website, most companies will send you a project brief form. I recommend that before filling this in you sit down and look through lots of websites that you like, which work on the model you need, and work out what's good about them. Is it the colour scheme, the content, the easy navigation? Doing this will help you think clearly about what you need.

Then make a map of your website on paper. What would be on each page? How would the pages link to each other? When talking to your designers you should think about …

- The goal of your site. Are you trying to get people to buy, sign up for membership, or refer you?
- Your target customers. How old are they, what are their online

habits, where do they hang out online?

- Show them five sites that you like and would like to emulate, and detail why you like them.
- Tell them what design concept you would like, including layout, logo, fonts, and colours. Obviously they are designing the site but you want to give them an idea of what you want so they can be creative.
- List the features you need – number of products, order and admin features, forums, reports, shopping cart, payment gateway.
- How many sales you expect. This is obviously going to be a guess but if it needs to be quickly scalable to accommodate much higher sales one day, the designer needs to know.
- Do you want to be able to edit the content yourself? You might want a site where you can update the content regularly, change the home-page message, or change product descriptions. You don't want to have to keep going back to the designer to make those changes; that will get expensive, fast.

## Hiring a Good Web Designer

A good web designer will understand your requirements and concept and will work towards your goals, and not just to expand their portfolio. Be aware though that some companies don't care if your website succeeds; they get paid anyway.

## Designers

You will find designers that either work individually on a freelance basis or work in a team within a company. Before you decide you need to establish some key points:

- Which one can provide most time and attention to your website and give ongoing support?
- Do they have the experience to give you what you want?
- If you are dealing with a company, can you speak directly to the designer?
- Can they meet your schedules? This means not only the initial

23

build, but can they update your site to accommodate things like promotions and special offers?

- What support to they offer? Is it 24/7? You want to know that if you have a problem or the site stops working that you can get it fixed quickly. Every hour your site isn't working or is down, you could be losing sales and customers might never come back.

Where possible, get them to sign a contract that specifies what they are providing, the delivery timescale for completion, the total cost of the project, and make sure that all intellectual property rights that make up the website are yours and yours alone. You definitely want to own your own website in case you fall out with the company – you don't want them owning everything if this happens.

You also want to know what's included in your deal.

- How much will they charge for the initial mock design and when will it be delivered?
- How many revisions of the mock-up do you get?
- How much will updates cost?
- If they do Search Engine Optimisation or SEO for short, how much does this cost? This is a method for making sure that search engines find you and rank you highly when giving results for searches. This is very important as you don't want to spend your life on page five of the results. No one ever looks that far.
- How much will hosting cost if they are hosting your site? I recommend you get it hosted elsewhere. If you fall out with the company you don't have to move your site as it already 'lives' elsewhere.
- How much will it cost to add or activate features after the initial build? You may want to do special promotions or sales periodically.

### Experience

You want to know what experience your potential design team have. Will they be using hard code with HTML? In other words, will they be building it from scratch from the bottom up using original code? If they are, they are very experienced. On the other hand, they may only use templates, which means they aren't experienced coders. While you may not want a site built from scratch, knowing your team can do it if necessary shows they have good skills. You may also find that even when using a template, some of the code needs to be tinkered with, so it's a good idea to get an experienced team.

Ask them to explain how they will optimise your site for SEO, or search engine optimisation, so that Google can find your site when someone searches for your keywords. You need to find a team that can answer your questions with passion and enthusiasm and make it easy for you to understand. Don't let them flannel you about what a dark art it is. It isn't easy and Google and other search engines and sites are always changing their algorithms to make it difficult for people to 'game' the system to get good page rankings. But the team should be able to explain some solid basics to you

### Mock Design

When you get your mock design make sure your designer uploads it to a live test site online. You then sit at home on your laptop and view it online just as a real customer would see it. This should also enable you to test the navigation, not just the appearance. Do the page links work? If you want to be able to click an image, does that work?

These are my top 5 tips for getting what you need.

1.  Don't hire an overly glitzy company – that will be expensive. But don't hire a mate who can build websites in his bedroom, either. You need ongoing support and you need it 24/7.
2.  Keep control of your website by having it hosted away from the design company. If you fall out with your designer they can't change your password and lock you out.
3.  Don't pay up-front. If they want a deposit, that's fine, and then you can pay in stages, but don't pay before you've seen the design or you may become stuck with one that doesn't work

for your business.
4. Remember, they won't be loyal to you. They will have other projects and you may not be their priority at any given time, especially if something bigger and shiner comes along from a client who is paying more.
5. Don't be afraid to walk away if you aren't happy.

## Off-the-Shelf Website Templates

It can often be worthwhile to start without the investment of a design company and use an off-the-shelf package that you can adapt. This can be a very sensible way to test an idea if you have some basic skills and can create good artwork for banners and logos. Companies offer different packages for various monthly payments, and as well as producing and managing your website they can also offer various features including promotions, discounts, and marketing. Accent Press's first website was created using a package like this.

There are several good companies that offer very adaptable sites – we use WordPress for most of our marketing blogs and Bluepark provided our first website.

## Chapter Five
## Domain Names

First things first, you need a name and you need a domain name or web address also known as a URL (Uniform Resource Locator – you don't need to remember this! Just think URL).

| TOP TIP |
| --- |
| This is one of the most important things you will do when setting up your website. Your web address and your name are a crucial part of your brand. Spend time getting this right! |

When naming your company it pays to find out whether that name is available as a domain name. You don't want to decide on calling your company Pansy Designs only to find that someone else has the domain names www.pansydesigns.com and www.pansydesigns.co.uk, even if they don't have a limited company. The company name may be available but every time someone tries to find you they'll end up on their site. And remember, if your company name is difficult to spell or has hyphens in it, it may be difficult for people to search for you online, so keep it simple.

### Keywords

Keywords are the words people use to search for something. For instance, if you are looking for blue gardening gloves, then a company with the URL www.bluegardeninggloves.co.uk is probably going to appear on the first page of Google.

Google indexes the entire content of your site and millions of other sites, and while it will find all your keywords buried in it, your domain name is still the biggest clue for a search engine as to whether your website is relevant to the search words a potential visitor has used.

There is disagreement among internet gurus about whether you should have your keywords in your domain name. I think it certainly makes sense if you don't have a big marketing budget to get your brand noticed. For instance, if people are looking for teddy bear kits then it might make sense to call your business www.teddybearkits.co.uk. This does work, but it may not be appropriate for your business. You may sell different types of products and so need different keywords. You may also sell doll kits. But many companies have several URLs that all 'point' to the same site. So you could have www.teddybearkits.co.uk and www.dollkits.co.uk that both point to your site. Your visitors would land on the appropriate page. On the other hand your URL doesn't always have to be the same as your business name. DIY giant B&Q website isn't www.bandq.co.uk, it's www.diy.co.uk.

Another reason for having your top keyword in your URL is that it will help you get incoming links; these are links from other website. The more links there are pointing from other websites to yours the better, it will push you up the Google rankings, which means you stand more chance of getting onto the first results page displayed on Google. People may link to your website because they think it's a good resource for their visitors if they deal with the same keywords.

**You Have a Name**

Once you have decided on a name you need to see if it's available. There are plenty of sites where you can check this – we use 123-reg.co.uk.

---

**TOP TIP**

When you are setting up a company, whether it's an internet company or not, you should try to choose a name for that company with an available domain name.

---

# All Domains are Not Created Equal

Let's start with Top Level Domains or TLDs as they're called. This deals with the last part of the address after the dot, that's the **.co.uk** or the **.com** or the **.org**

A TLD identifies something about the website such as its purpose, the organisation that owns it, or the geographical area where it originates.

Country code TLDs show you where a website is, so if you are in the UK it's **.co.uk**, or if you are in New Zealand it's **.co.nz**

Other TLDs like **.org** and **.net** tend to be used by specific sectors. Charities and Not-For-Profit enterprises often use **.org**, with techie companies it's **.net**, and UK academic institutions will be **.ac.uk**

This isn't fixed, there's no internet police to stop you using **.net** even if you were a florist, but it wouldn't be a good idea.

If you're aiming for the UK market only then it makes sense to choose a **.co.uk** for your site. But if you're after a wider audience then you'll need the **.com**.

**.com** is the most common TLD and it is *always* worth getting this, even if you use **.co.uk** too, because you can point them both at your website. Be aware, you don't want someone setting up a **.com** with the same name as your **.co.uk**.

There are less popular TLDs like **.me.uk**, or **.biz.tv**, but I'd avoid these if you can. You would need a really good reason to use them. You don't want your flourishing nappy delivery service www.happynappy.me.uk to get confused with a rival on www.happynappy.com.

If you are selling to Europe you could try the **.eu** TLD but **.com** will always have higher credibility.

If your chosen domain name is gone, check to see whether the owner of that name is actually using it. They might be persuaded to sell it if they bought it and it's lying idle or is hardly used.

## Careful of Spelling!

Be very careful that your company name doesn't spell something else when written with no spaces between the words as a web address. Here are some examples of how that can go horribly wrong.

- A site for celebrity agents called 'Who Represents'. That sounds pretty straightforward, doesn't it? What's their domain name?

  www.whorepresents.com

- Do you often find yourself in need of a biro? You could go to Pen Island.

  www.penisland.net

- Perhaps you need a therapist? Therapist Finder is a 'does what it says on the tin' kind of name, isn't it?

  www.therapistfinder.com

Maybe not!

You get the point. With no spaces, things read very differently.

One way of avoiding this is to add a hyphen, but only if it's the only way to get the perfect name – they show up lower in Google rankings than non-hypenated names.

Once you have decided on a name and it doesn't contain any embarrassing mistakes then you should register that address. There are plenty of sites where you can do this, such as http://www.123-reg.co.uk. Once it's registered, you own that domain name for the length of the contract, usually one or two years. You then renew it as required, no one can take it away from you unless you let the contract lapse.

---

**TOP TIP**

Don't register your domain with the hosting company you are going to use. If you face any problems with them in the future you may find it awkward to move your domain name. Always keep control of your domain name and keep it with your domain registrar.

---

## Who Owns It?

If your company becomes very successful then your URL will become valuable, so be careful who registers it. If you want it to be linked to your limited company then register it with that company. If you want to own it personally, then register it personally.

## Register a Few

Domain names, particularly **.co.uk**, are very cheap these days, so register several combinations of your name, including things you might need in the future. It won't cost much and it will give you flexibility and insurance against potential rivals.

**Chapter Six**
**Hosting – A Home for Your Website**

Now, before you think of diving in to build a website let's pause to take a look at other essential elements you will need to consider.

In this section we're going to look at how to find the right host for your site and how to build it. We'll also consider design and content to get visitors wanting to buy from you.

Your online business doesn't just need a website, it needs a website that *works*, technically and aesthetically.

Your website is made up of text, images, and media files which will all be stored on a server. Your visitors will view it through a browser like Mozilla Firefox, Internet Explorer, or Safari. In very simple language, your website is like a dynamic document that a visitor opens, which means it needs to be stored in place they can get to it easily. So where your website 'lives' is pretty important.

Sites are stored on servers; these are computers designed to process requests and deliver data to other computers over the internet or a local network.

There are three different choices when it comes to storing your site.

Dedicated Servers

This is a server that's dedicated entirely to your website. It is also much more expensive than shared hosting. If you are expecting large volumes of traffic, have lots of images or videos, or have particular security needs, then you will need dedicated hosting on an individual server. Also, if you are developing a web application, in other words if your product is delivered to the customer via the internet and isn't a physical product, then this is your best choice. You get complete control over your server with administrator-level access. Your own server will get you as close to 100% uptime as possible.

Uptime is the amount of time a website is online. Nothing is ever perfect and there are always blips, but you want your website visible as close to 100% of the time as possible.

Shared Servers

This is the cheapest option and the easiest to set up. You're not in control of the server, you are just uploading your files to it. There is potential for your site's performance to be affected by the volume of traffic the server has to cope with. If one of the other sites on that server suddenly gets a huge amount of traffic this could affect your site.

This is, however, the most sensible option for most businesses as it's much cheaper and you probably don't have enough technical know-how yet to take advantage of having your own server. There's a huge variety of packages out there at variable prices.

Virtual Private Servers (VPS)

These are halfway between a dedicated and a shared server. Without getting too technical it's basically a computer running 'virtual servers' – so they're not separate servers but they behave like they're separate and are treated as separate by the computer. But you will get less hard disk space, and performance will be lower. It can offer a compromise between shared and dedicated though.

**The Right Host**

Finding the right hosting company for your new business is very important. You are paying them to store your website on their server, which is on their premises, and to make sure it is connected to the internet so that potential viewers can get to it with their browsers.

The right host can make sure you're site has maximum uptime and loads quickly onto a potential customer's computer or phone. Slow loading makes people impatient and they bounce off to your competitors.

---

**WARNING!**

Choose the wrong hosting company and you'll be tearing your hair out when your site goes down and you can't get hold of the company's customer support to sort it out. Or you could find it takes so long for your site to load that those potential customers

---

you've worked so hard to bring to your site get fed up after 15 seconds and go elsewhere.

You need to find a reputable host for your website. Ask some other businesspeople whom they use for their sites and what their experience is.

When you are choosing a hosting company make sure you get the following …

- Good Bandwidth
- Good Load Speed
- Rapid Support
- Maximum Uptime

Most hosting companies offer a variety of bandwidth options in their plans. Hosting packages usually include a certain amount of hard disk space. How much you get is usually reflected in how much you pay. But most websites don't need a lot of space so don't assume you need a huge amount. Most sites will fit into a few hundred megabytes. So don't be lured in by offers of 'unlimited space'; you might not need it.

Bandwidth

Most hosting companies offer a variety of bandwidth options in their plans. So exactly what is bandwidth? It's the amount of traffic that is allowed between your website and the rest of the internet.

The amount of bandwidth any hosting company can give you depends on their network connections, both internal to their own data centre and external to the internet.

How does it work? Let's look first at the size of the data that bounces around from your host to the internet. Data is measured in bytes, which is the name for a unit of digital information in computing. If you send photos across in emails you will know that if they have a huge number of bytes they may be so big that they don't send easily. Byte sizes go up from bytes to kilobytes, megabytes, gigabytes, and the largest, terabytes. These descriptions of size are usually shortened to KB, MB, GB, TB.

So, back to bandwidth, and why it's important. If you have a web page that contains 100KB of data, then each time someone views that page they're using 100KB of your bandwidth allowance. So if you don't have enough bandwidth your website won't work very well.

So how much will you need? Most small business sites will not need more than 1GB of bandwidth per month. If your site is made up of static web pages and you expect little traffic to your site on a daily basis, go with a low-bandwidth plan. If you go over the amount of bandwidth allocated in your plan, your hosting company could charge you over-usage fees, so if you think the traffic to your site will be significant, you may want to opt for plan that allows you to go higher. Talk to your hosting company and be realistic about what traffic you expect. Can you upgrade easily? Will they warn you if you are about to hit your usage ceiling?

Load Speed

You also want your website to load quickly. If it takes too long, potential visitors will just go elsewhere. None of us have much patience on the web! One way to keep load time to a minimum is to reduce the size and amount of images on your site.

Maximum Uptime

Uptime is the amount of time that a server has stayed up and running. This is usually listed as a percentage, like '99.9% uptime.' It's a good measure of how good a Web hosting provider is at keeping their systems up and running. You need to make sure your website is live 24/7 and that if it goes down they will fix it quickly. While your site is down you are potentially losing money.

## Get the Right Service

If you are going to go for the dedicated hosting option or the VPS then make sure you find a provider with a guaranteed 'service level'. I have mentioned above that you should get 99.9% of uptime. Why is this important? Well, imagine if it's only 99%. That may sound almost perfect but what if it means is that your site could be 'down' for up to seven hours a month. That's almost a whole working day.

If you have shared hosting, the company is much less likely to quote you a figure of the uptime. So how do you check it? Well, I would ring their helpdesk and ask them. How quickly and how well they answer you will tell you a great deal about their service!

If they can't give you a guaranteed figure, then ask them for their average over the last year. You can't expect 99.9% because it's shared and you are paying less, but it's worth seeing what the figure is.

## Options for Hosting

Many hosting sites also provide site-creation tools, which are basically editable templates you can use. Now, this does have some limitations but it does mean you can get a functioning site up quickly, and most modern templates look professional. Try www.1and1.co.uk or uk.godaddy.com/.

Many hosting sites like these offer a free trial so you can see whether or not the interface works for you.

---

**TOP TIP**

If you are given the option of monthly payments rather than quarterly or annual, take the monthly option to begin with so you can check out how good the hosting company is. If you have a dedicated server you may be asked to sign up for a year. Be very careful of signing a long contract before you know how reliable the hosting company is. You don't want to get locked in to a contract with a hosting company that turns out to be rubbish.

---

## Emails

Make sure your package includes enough email addresses. You don't want to use a personal email address. If you are running a business then a Gmail or a Hotmail account will make you look like an amateur. You may be a one-man-band but you don't want to make that obvious. You can have several email addresses that all come to you.

For instance:
yourname@mybusiness.co.uk
customersupport@mybusiness.co.uk
info@mybusiness.co.uk
contact@mybusiness.co.uk

## Chapter Seven
## Writing the Content

One of the classic mistakes that many people make when building their website is to spend all their time on the design and forget how important the words are, then fling blocks of text in without too much thought.

The look and feel of your website is very important but so is the information. It's especially important on your home page and on the other landing pages.

Landing pages are ones where your visitors 'land' first. If your company www.bestcosmetics.co.uk sells all types of cosmetics, then your visitor might get taken straight to your mascaras page if the search words she has used are 'waterproof mascara'. She won't get taken from Google to the home page. So the text or 'copy' on your pages has to be good.

### Writing is Hard

You may be no good at writing persuasive copy. And that's fine, not everyone is an advertising copywriter. It's perfectly acceptable and is very often a good idea to hire a copywriter to do the job for you. But even if you do that remember that it's YOUR website so it's your responsibility to get it right. The copywriter doesn't know your business like you do, so make sure they have a good idea before they write a single sentence. You can't just bundle off the job to a professional scribbler and expect it to come back perfect. It has to be right for your visitors if you are going to turn them into customers.

| TOP TIP |
| --- |
| Your copy is your message – Your message is your business!<br>So define what your message is before you start writing. |

You should be doing most of the work and the copywriter should be polishing it. But how do you know what information to put down?

Who is your Customer?

If you don't know who your customer is then don't write anything. Find out who your customer is first before you compose any copy at all. Many newbies write their web copy for themselves, but remember; it's not for you, it's for your potential customers.

When someone comes to your website they're asking themselves if your website can do anything for them. Are you solving a problem, making life easier, giving them more time, or just making life more pleasurable for them? Thousands of people may come to your site but each person has his or her individual needs.

Anticipate your audience's needs and write to that. Tell them what the benefits of your products and services are to them, don't just describe the features.

---

**TATTOO THIS ON YOUR FOREHEAD!**

People don't buy features, they buy *benefits*. Would you buy a mascara with a curved wand designed and inspired by Japanese car technology? Or would you buy a mascara that makes your lashes look lush, long, full, and won't run, even in a hurricane?

---

Headlines are good place to push the benefits of your products. They are the most important lines in your copy as they stand out and are the first thing people read. If the headline grabs them they'll read the rest. If it doesn't? That's obvious!

If you need inspiration there are lots of sites on the internet listing some of the most successful types of headlines. Many of the tried and tested ones start with *'How to ...'* something or other. *How to Win Friends and Influence People* is the most famous example. It's one of the best-selling self-help books of all time. Or how about *'The Secret to ...'* followed by whatever your secret is, perhaps it's *'... better skin'*, or a *'... bigger income'*.

### What Should Your Visitor Do?

You should have a very clear idea of what you want your visitor to do. Do you want them to buy something, sign up for a newsletter, or ring for a consultation?

| **TOP TIP** |
|:---:|
| If it isn't obvious, they won't do it! |

What do I mean by obvious? Well, it has to be easy to do, you have to make it a no-brainer, and you have to make it visible. There are so many different sizes of screen out there, from an enormous 30-inch Mac screen to a smartphone. The action you want them to take should be near the top so they don't have to scroll down.

Whatever it is you want them to do, whether it's 'Sign Up' or 'Buy Now', make sure that button can be placed at around 500 pixels down the page. This should cover most computers. But if you are targeting mobile users you will have to place it higher and test your site on different devices.

### Clarity, Simplicity, and Grammar

It seems obvious but make sure your grammar and spelling are accurate. With grammar and spellcheckers this isn't difficult these days. Nothing will make your site look amateurish more quickly than bad English.

If your copy is sloppy, what will your service be like? What will your product be like? That's what a potential customer will be thinking subconsciously.

Be ruthless in your copy editing. Check every word to see if you need it. If it doesn't add to your message and doesn't push people to the action you want them to take, you don't need it. Keep re-reading it and ask yourself if your visitors really need to know what you've included.

### Be Relevant for Google

Google will rank you according to your relevance to web searches. Simple. So you want to be relevant. How does Google decide? It looks at the keywords in your content and the links to you. As I've said, keywords are the words that people use to search for what they want in a search engine. So the keywords that people would use to search for you should be in the content of your website.

You may have heard people say that you can just cram your copy with keywords, but that doesn't work, Google is wise to that. And be warned, if you do that, you can end up blacklisted, then you're finished. So you have to write your copy for real people, not just the search engines.

Good keywords are critical for …

- Your organic traffic. The people who come to your site through a search engine like Google.
- The success of a Google AdWords advertising campaign.
- Your Google ranking.
- Amazon and eBay ranking

But making your pages attractive to Google isn't just a case of packing them with keywords. You need to assess your keywords carefully.

The biggest rookie mistake people make is to use keywords that are almost right; that is, they are close to the term people use to search but not exactly the same. So choose your words wisely and precisely. You should start with a small set of highly focused keywords. Don't write a long list of words and try to use them all, it will just confuse you. In most AdWords advertising campaigns the most profitable clicks come from just a few of your keywords.

### How Do You Choose Keywords?

Begin with your main keywords, the ones you may have used in your domain name, your company name, or blog. So if your site is call www.buyhotpointspares.co.uk then your key phrase is 'Hotpoint spares'.

---

**TOP TIP**

Use Google's keyword tool to help you find a list of good related keywords: www.google.co.uk/keywordplanner
Type your main keyword or keyword phrase into the box.
Check the box that asks you to show only results that are closely related to your search terms.

---

Google will show you terms related to your keyword and you'll see what volume that search generates.

## \<H\> Tags

Google likes it when you give it a clue as to what you think is important on each page of your website. The way to do this is to use Header or 'H' tags in the code of your website, in the HTML. When you put words in a header you are telling Google 'This is the important bit!' So once you've decided what's important, make sure your web designer puts headers into the code of your site.

A Header is a sign to the search engine that the text is important, a headline if you like. It's like making a sentence bold or underlined. You may have made the text look like it has been put in bold or underlined but the search engine isn't looking at its appearance. It gets a clue from the code.

So you have to sort your Headers in order of relevance. If you have three main points you want to flag up to the search engines then your Header tags will be H1, H2, H3, and so on.

## Chapter Eight
## Search Engine Optimisation

If you want people to find you through organic searches (from entering keywords in a search engine), then you need to optimise your site with SEO. Many see it as a dark and mysterious art. There are many specialist companies around who promise to be able to cast a magic spell over your site. But it's a good idea to understand the basics as you can do an awful lot to help yourself. And the more you know the less likely it will be that someone will sell you smoke and mirrors.

There are No Guarantees

Any company that tells you they can guarantee to get you a Page One ranking for high-traffic keywords is fibbing.

It Takes Time

SEO takes time, you can't hurry it along. Google likes older sites and will rank them more highly than new kids on the block. You also get bonus points for having incoming links to your site if they're relevant and from highly-ranked sites. But these take time to accumulate.

### Optimising Your Web Copy

The copy you write on your website doesn't have to appeal to just your visitors, it also needs to appeal to Google. Search engines like relevance and that's what they reward. The closer your copy matches the phrases used to search for what people want, the higher up the rankings you will go. So you have to structure your copy in a way that takes advantage of that.

### Your Pages

Each page should deal with specific content as search engines link to an entire page. If you have too many subjects on one page then the density of keywords on that page will be lower.

## Structure

Think about the main message of each page. What are you trying to say? Keep your content relevant to that message.

Also think about where you are putting the most important information. When you look at a web page, monitor how you read it. Most people look for information at the top then at the bottom and gloss over the middle. Google has worked this out and gives more weight to the wording at the top and the bottom, so put your keywords in there.

## HTML

Short for HyperText Markup Language, this is 'language' that's used to create documents on the web. It describes the meaning of the content, not how it looks. In very rough terms think of it as the workings of a washing machine and not the shiny front with all the flashing lights.

It has tags which define the structure and layout of a page.

For instance a heading tag which looks like this <h> shows that this is the most important text on the page. So Google gives more weight to the words in here. So your keywords need to be in here.

Don't be tempted to write a clever heading with no keywords. It may work in a novel but it won't impress Google.

If someone is designing your website, talk to them about your keywords and give them a list so they know what's important to put in certain tags. But bear in mind, you are trying to impress human eyes as well as Google's. So don't optimise your site to the point where it reads really badly.

## Images

Images will also affect how your site is optimised. You should attach alternative text to your image. The Google spiders that search through sites will read this alternative text. Google also reads the name of the image, so make sure you have your keywords in the names of the images, putting hyphens between the words. That way both your visitors and Google will be able to read it. I will look at this in more detail in the next chapter.

## Metatags

Once upon a time you could fool Google into believing what you wanted them to believe by putting information in a metatag, which is in the source code. Originally they were intended as a way of search engines getting information about the site. But search engines have moved on and now use the content to do that. So metatags don't have any effect on your SEO any more.

The only metatag you should worry about is the 'Description' tag. The text you put in here will come up under the heading on a search page. If you haven't filled it in, then the search engine will just grab some copy from your web page to display.

## Title Tag

Again, this tag appears in your HTML coding. You must make sure your <title> tag is correct. This will appear in the browser's title bar. Use your main keywords in your title tag which will boost your ranking.

## Links

Google loves incoming links to your site, so you should aim to get links from good sites with good rankings. Don't just get links for the sake of it, make them quality links. Are they really relevant to your site? As I said, Google likes relevance. It also likes established sites, so the older the site you get a link from the better.

Outgoing links, or links on your site to other sites, don't really affect your ranking but they may provide value for your visitors. Be careful not to let them navigate away from your site, though. If you are providing links make sure they 'Open in New Window' which means another window will open for that website. When the visitor has had enough they close the window and they are still on your site.

## Chapter Nine
## Images and Graphics

A picture speaks a thousand words. We all know that. If one of your friends posts an update on Facebook you are more likely to 'Comment' or 'Like' if it has an image attached. We all are. We like images.

But when we talk about website 'content', we're usually talking about the words. We focus on headlines and calls to action, the product descriptions, and the 'About Us' pages. We should be paying a great deal of attention to other stuff, the images, graphics, and increasingly the audio and video content. We will talk about audio and video in chapters ten and seventeen. For now let's focus on static images.

What's the first thing you notice when you look at a new website? It's almost certainly the images. But they're often overlooked when planning a new site.

We are all quite web-savvy these days, we can tell pretty quickly if a site is good or not and whether it works or not, and the images play a big part in our snap decision-making. We can identify images that don't help us and the ones that do. The implication of this is that if a site is has images on it that are just there for decoration or to 'fill' the page, it won't encourage your visitors to do what you want them to do. At best those images will take up valuable space, at worst they'll annoy and frustrate visitors and they'll bounce away. And when they bounce away that's a potential sale lost.

The quality of your photographs is really important. Think about how you shop online. You can't touch or look closely at the products. You can't feel them, smell them, or walk around them. So the image is all you have. If you want people to buy from you then your images have to be high quality. Don't be tempted to take photos with your camera-phone, invest in high quality, high resolution shots, which are well-lit and done professionally. Do this even if the image is of you rather than products. If *you* are the brand, then make it a high quality brand.

If you are selling products bear these points in mind when planning your images.

- Highlight important details and differences in products.
- Shoot from different angles, so your visitors get a really good look at the product.
- If there are textures, patterns, or intricate details then make sure there's a zoom function on the images or close-up shots.
- Use live action shots, showing the products being used by real people. This especially applies to clothes; show them on models.
- If your products have options, such as colours or added extras, then show all of the available options, don't just give a list of colours and features.

## Graphics

Graphic design elements can be used for stylistic reasons but also used as instructions. Think of stylized arrows or buttons to direct your visitors to important information. Accent Press uses a small sliding banner about a third of the way down our homepage which showcases our different series of books, providing customers with our range of products from the moment they land on our site.

Make sure you are careful of these, though, as they can end up cluttering up your site and annoying your visitors. Use them sparingly or it will make it harder to navigate your site, not easier.

## Diagrams

Sometimes illustrations and diagrams can be more useful in explaining your products than a block of text or images. They may not be as attractive as a full-colour photo, but they might be more useful to your visitor. For instance, if you are running a site called www.solarpanels4u.co.uk then you might want to show a graph detailing energy use to illustrate how much money visitors could save if they bought your solar panels. A clear visual image of a saving is very often more easily and quickly understood than a list

of costs or percentages.
If you are going to use graphics consider these tips.

- Stay consistent. Any graphics should blend in style and colour with the rest of your site.
- Show what's important and keep it simple. A cluttered or complicated graphic is not going to help your visitor. What you are trying to show them has to be obvious.
- Don't use graphics instead of text. If a graphic is the only thing on the site that explains your Unique Selling Point (USP) to the customer then how is Google going to find it? You can put alternative text in which shows up if people have the image function turned off and Google reads this. But you still need keywords in your text.

---

**TOP TIP**
Make sure your web designer adds alternative text for your graphics and images.

---

### Alternative Text

Alternative text is used for several reasons. It is used in place of images for visitors with visual impairment. It is also displayed instead of the image by browsers that don't support images or when a visitor has chosen not to display images.

It provides a meaning and description for the images which can be read by search engines. So the text has to show both the *content* and the *function* of the images.

### When Should I use Graphics and Images?

Websites with no graphics or images at all are pretty dull. But you must be careful not to overuse them. There are three basic reasons to use them.

- Branding
- Decoration
- Illustration

If you are thinking of using an image or a graphic and it doesn't fall into one of these categories, then ask yourself why you are using it. Even if it's for decoration, remember that it's taking up space and if it isn't working towards making people want to buy your services or products then it isn't working at all. Every image, graphic, and word on your website has to earn its space.

## Branding

Your logo is important: it's your brand. My erotic books brand is called Xcite Books and the logo is a large **X** with the letters **cite** under it: It's the X on the book covers that people notice and that makes it obvious that the content is not for those who blush easily.

## Logos

You have probably starting dreaming about what kind of logo you want. You might have started doodling on notepads and playing with the colours you like. But if you aren't a graphic designer you will need to outsource this job. If you're strapped for cash and you are bootstrapping your business (that's business-speak for doing things on a shoestring, quite literally), then you can try a freelance site like www.fiverr.com or www.elance.com.

These are websites where freelancers bid for jobs that are posted by people who need work done. The advantage of these sites is that a worldwide audience of freelancers see the job and can bid for it, so there is an army of talent out there. But you may have to wade through a lot of bids and a lot of rubbish before you choose one. Now this is a cheap option and it may work for you but you could also be disappointed. So bear in mind you may have to go to a UK company and pay a little more.

If you don't know where to go then look around for logos you like or that reflect the kind of image you want and find out who designed them. It may not be wise to look at huge brands who may have paid thousands for a designer, but there will be plenty of smaller brands, even local shops, that have great logos.

A professional designer should ask you lots of questions about what you want. As with the web designers, be prepared to give them a proper 'brief' or you will be disappointed and charged for something you can't use. You can ask for changes, but within reason. You should speak to the designer and not an agency as you need to convey exactly what you want to the person who is designing it.

Remember that the colours of your logo will reflect the image you want and that your site should blend with it. You don't want a logo that doesn't appear to fit on your site because the colours and styles clash.

### Decoration

Be very, very careful with this category and ask yourself why the image needs to be there. If it is a background graphic behind the text then it is not taking up valuable space, but make sure it doesn't just clutter up your site or make it difficult to read.

If you need images, then make sure you source the images correctly. Don't be tempted to rip them from another website. You may not have the right to use them and the quality will be dreadful. There are plenty of sites that will sell you stock images or clipart and they won't break the bank. Try www.shutterstock.com www.istockphoto.com or www.thinkstockphotos.co.uk.

You can either buy individual images or you can set up a subscription if you are going to need regular new content. We use ThinkStock at Accent Press, and as we need access to a large amount of images for our book covers, we have an annual subscription that allows us to download up to 25 images a day. You, however, may have different needs. You don't need to keep the subscription for long. You can choose all your images, subscribe for a month, and download everything you need in one go.

When you save images you want to save them at the exact size you want them to appear on your site in pixels. If you don't the quality will suffer when browsers downsize them. There are three file formats widely used on websites – JPEG, PNG, and GIF.

Your default choice should be JPEG. It compresses better than PNG and supports more colours than GIF.

If you aren't familiar with manipulating images then it would be better to talk to your website developer, who will be able to do this for you.

## Illustration

If you are selling products then you will need images to show them. If you are selling services you might want images to illustrate this, either stock shots or photos of you working with customers. If you have a product that needs an explanation then you might want a diagram. If you are selling a service that needs to illustrate something like growth, for instance you're a marketing advisor, then you might want to include a graph that shows the average increase in sales for the clients you work with.

---

**TOP TIP**

If you have no professional photos don't be tempted to take your own, even with a good camera, unless you have the skill and the kit to achieve professional results. Your photos are a reflection of how good and how professional you are. Bad photos will make it look as if the products are rubbish or that you are an amateur. That's the not the image that's going to make you money.

---

## Chapter Ten
## Videos and Audio

We're all familiar with YouTube and how video content is now used to sell just about everything. Used well, video or audio can really enhance your site. But get it wrong and your potential customers will bounce away from you in seconds.

The first thing to bear in mind is the circumstances your visitors will find themselves in when they visit your site. Are they at home? Are they on a train? Are they at work? If your video or sound files open automatically when they land on your website that means they have no control over it. If someone is sitting at their desk at lunchtime they might not want their interest in my website selling erotic novels www.xcitebooks.co.uk broadcast all over the office!

So if you are going to include media files of any kind make sure that your visitor has the choice over whether to play them or not.

Videos are effective if they are there for a very specific purpose. They're usually used on landing pages when someone is looking for something specific. Video and audio are rarely used effectively on home pages. A video explaining how to use a product might work well on the product page. If you offer a service and you are the service, you may want to put a short message on video on the home page, but otherwise there needs to be a very good reason for having video on the home page.

### Hosting Your Video or Audio

If you are creating a video or audio that will be useful both on and off your site, like a marketing video, then it would be sensible to host it away from your own site on another site like YouTube.

You can still embed that video on your site using the links that YouTube provide. All you have to do is upload your media content, and then once it's live you copy and paste their 'Embed' code into your HTML code on your site.

If your media content is for your website only then store it in your own web space.

## What Kind of Media?

You can use video or just sound on your site, it depends what you are trying to achieve. Using just sound is less common but may work for your site.

## Video

Videos on websites are usually either a person talking to the viewer or a demonstration. Let's have a look at the talking head, which is often used by internet gurus or people selling themselves as a consultant or expert. It works well if you don't have a physical product to sell.

This can be very effective, but only if done well. You have to inspire friendliness and confidence, so keep your speech short so that you don't end up rambling or trying to remember a long script you've written.

The second type is a product demonstration which is only really necessary if it's the only way you can show the benefits of the product. If you are selling kitchen gadgets, then a video showing how much time and effort they will save the buyer would be a bonus. Think of all those things you have in your kitchen cupboards that a TV demo persuaded you to buy!

Whatever the purpose of your video you have to make it look professional unless you are going for a more urban-cool look. If you are selling skateboards then you might want it shot in a quirky style that looks a little more D.I.Y.

Use a good camcorder, preferably one with a screen that shows you what you are recording. Put it on a tripod for steadiness and make sure your scene is well-lit.

Get the sound right. It's no good having great pictures if you can hardly hear what's being said. If your camcorder has a mic input socket then a lapel mic will work. Make sure you don't leave the black lead dangling down your front as you're speaking, tuck it in so that only the mic itself is showing. Also remember not to turn your head away from it when you are talking as you will sound 'off-mic'.

If you don't have a mic socket then you may have to record your audio on a separate machine. Try a Zoom H2 Handy recorder. This will set you back quite a bit but if you are going to be recording a lot of audio then it's worth it. You will have to synchronise your video and audio when you edit. You can either find software that lets you do this in the edit, or you can do it yourself when you're recording. We're all familiar with the clapper board we see on movies when they start a take. Do your own. When you are recording, clap loudly so that the camcorder sees you doing it and the sound recorder captures it. That way, when you come to edit you will be able to line up the two sources.

**Editing**

If you have a Mac then iMovie will edit your video perfectly well, and it's quite simple to use. Alternatively, there are various editing programs available like Adobe Premiere Elements or Magix Movie Edit Pro. You will have to buy this software but if you are going to be using a lot of video or changing your video content regularly then it will be worth investing in the kit and learning how to use it.

As connection speeds increase, video is becoming more commonplace throughout the web, especially in e-commerce. Recent research shows there's a boost in traffic and higher conversions for online retailers that include product videos. But don't add a video just for the sake of video. As with product images, users can quickly identify whether it's meaningful or simply padding, and they'll respond accordingly.

Videos can be especially helpful for showcasing products in action. Customers want to know how a product works, so show them with video. For example, if you sell D.I.Y. tools, you could create a series of videos showing customers how to do certain D.I.Y. jobs using those tools. You could also put these videos on YouTube as an educational channel which will bring people to your site. Using product videos in this way shows your products in action, and it creates traffic to your site through people searching for answers then sharing them with social media. I'll be discussing YouTube videos more in Chapter Seventeen.

You can also use video for product testimonials and reviews. If you meet your customers ask them if you can record a testimonial or invite your customers to send them in.

Here are some tips on creating video for your site:

- Don't skimp on quality. Out of focus, badly shot, or choppy video doesn't make a good impression. If the video is bad, your products or service will look bad.
- Pay attention to the sound. Are you recording near a noisy road or can you hear a school playground in the background? Record somewhere quiet unless the background noise is relevant. You want the audience to hear you and listen to you.
- Go slow and steady. Don't be tempted to be flashy, tilting and panning and moving the camera around, you'll make your audience seasick. Put the camera on a tripod and keep all movements slow and steady.
- Share your videos. Once you've produced a great video, share it on YouTube, social media, and anywhere else you think potential customers will find it.

### Audio

Audio files are smaller than video files so they download more quickly. If you are selling products to visually-impaired customers then this may well be a media type that would work for you.

It also works well for certain types of products. You may be selling audio courses or products to do with sound such as natural sound effects to help people sleep. Perhaps you are selling music or promoting bands.

But even if you aren't selling any of these you can still use sound on your site. Just don't be tempted to use sound for the sake of it. Don't put background music on your site. If it opens automatically then we have just lost a potential customer – remember that person surfing the net at lunchtime in the office? And apart from that, it's just going to be annoying to your visitor, who will almost certainly never come to your site again.

Make sure your potential customers can open the sound sample files only when they want to.

If you want to use a voiceover on your site, the same applies;

don't have it come on automatically. You need a very good reason for using voiceover. If you are selling software you might need to show a screen shot and have a voiceover describing how the software works. Whatever the reason for using a voiceover, make sure you write a script, or if you feel confident speaking naturally make sure you have sound editing software to remove any mistakes or hesitations like 'ums' and 'ers'.

If you are recording the speech at home then you will need a good microphone, one that doesn't need a mixer. You can now buy good-quality mics that plug straight into your computer.

USB mics are relatively affordable. But they can be difficult to set up so make sure you have access to someone who can set it up for you if you're not confident you can do it yourself. This kind of mic provides above-average sound and works well for low-budget podcasting or short voiceovers.

If your ultimate goal is to record the best sounding voiceover possible, then you might have to pay for professional recording. People only notice sound quality when the quality is bad. USB mics won't have that warm sound that radio broadcasts have as those are done on different types of mic.

To edit your voiceover you will need sound editing software such as CoolEdit from Adobe. If you aren't going to be editing a lot of sound then you could try free open-source software such as audacity.sourceforge.net.

Here are some tips for creating audio for your site.

- Pay attention to the background. As with video, go somewhere quiet. Background noise is even more distracting when there are no pictures to provide context.
- Write out a script. A polished script helps you sound more professional and ensures you don't leave out any important details. But don't be tempted to sound clever by making it too wordy. Try to imagine you are just talking to your audience and use everyday language.
- Keep it small. Use MP3s instead of WAV files or other media formats to keep the file size down.

# Section Three

# Revenue Models

## Chapter Eleven
## How Are You Going to Make Money?

The same rules of business that apply to brick-and-mortar businesses apply to internet ones. At the end of the day, it's about selling something to someone.

If you only ask yourself one question when you start a business this should be it: how are you going to make money? If you haven't worked out what your revenue model is going to be, then you will be running round in circles, being very busy but not running a business.

The web has been around long enough now for there to be a great many ways to make money on it so let's look at a few.

### Selling Products

I'm sure you've bought things online, from Amazon, eBay, or a thousand other shops that either live entirely online or also have High Street outlets.

So in many ways this is a natural choice for an online business. You may have products in mind already. Or you may need to go looking for the right products to sell.

When you sell online, the same rule applies to virtual business as it does to physical shops. You must buy in your goods for a much lower price than you sell them. The difference in the price, or margin, has to be enough to pay all of your business expenses and still make a profit. So even if you sell your own hand-thrown pottery, you need to make enough money to cover the cost of electricity, buying a kiln, marketing, accountancy, web hosting, and all the other things that go along with running a business.

You have to ask yourself basic business questions:
- How much does producing or buying the products cost?
- How much is customs and tax going to cost if you're bringing them in from abroad?

- How much will shipping cost?
- What will fulfilment cost be – that is, how much will it cost you in postage and packing to get the goods to your customers?
- What volume of products do you need to sell to reach the profit margins you want?
- What are my extra expenses, like utilities, legal fees, insurance, and accountancy?

Then you need to ask yourself some e-commerce questions.

- How much traffic will you have to drive to your website and what will your conversation rate be? The conversion rate is the percentage of visitors that actually go on to buy something from you.
- How much money will you have to spend on marketing to get people to come to your site?

At the end of the day it's quite hard to quantify how much you are going to sell as it depends on the products themselves and how well you do your marketing. If you decide to go this route you must be absolutely certain there's a market for the products and that you believe in them.

### Buying Products to Sell

Don't worry if you can't or don't want to create your own products, because you don't have to. Most people who sell goods online buy them in and sell them on. And you have a choice of how to sell them. You can either sell them from your own website with a shopping cart or you can sell them through another website like Amazon or eBay.

If you sell from your own website then you don't to pay any extra costs to a middle-man. You get all the profits but you also have to do all the work. The marketing, postage, packing, and shipping are all up to you.

If you have absolutely no experience of selling and the idea of being responsible for all the physical stuff worries you, then you might want to start by allowing other sites to market your products. You would still have a website, but you wouldn't have to do anywhere near as much work. A site like eBay will allow you to create a shopfront for your products.

However you decide to sell, you still have to find your products in the first place. There are three basic ways to do this:

- Drop shipping
- Sourcing your own products
- Buying from a wholesaler

## Drop Shipping

I will talk about drop shipping first as for many first time online entrepreneurs it offers an easy way in to the world of e-commerce.

Drop shippers are companies that offer a range of products. You choose the products you want to sell and buy them from the drop shipper at wholesale prices. The drop shipper stores the products and ships them out to the customer when you make a sale. You are only charged by the drop shipper for that product when you make a sale, so you don't have to buy in expensive stock or store it.

The advantage of this system is that you don't need to have a warehouse, you don't need to invest in stock, and you don't need to worry about fulfilment. The drop shipper handles all of this for you and the system is only set in motion when a customer places an order.

So, the customer comes to your site and places an order. Once the payment has cleared you forward the order to your drop shipper and pay them the wholesale fee for the product. The drop shipper then sends out the product. The profit you make is the difference between what your customer paid you and what you pay the drop shipper. (Don't forget you will still need to make enough profit to cover your normal business expenses.)

The customer has no idea that the products didn't come from your warehouse. If you have chosen a good and reliable drop shipper then you benefit from their efficiency and customer service.

What you have to focus on is marketing and sales. You do all the front end and the drop shipper does all the back end: the stuff that happens after the customer has placed an order.

This all sounds wonderful, doesn't it? It can be a very profitable model, but there are downsides and you must be aware of them.

Anything that takes all the time and effort out of running a business is going to cost money. Drop shippers are not charities. So their 'cut' is going to be substantial. And, because you aren't buying in volume, the wholesale price they offer you may not be that good. That may push you into pricing your goods higher than other people are offering them for. And when you are paying more for your products you need an awful lot more customers to make money, so that means spending money on marketing to drive traffic to your website.

There are things you *must* be aware of before you go down this route.

Shipping – You won't have any control over the packaging or delivery dates, so discuss this with the drop shipper. You want to make sure that both are consistent with your company image.

Out of Stock – You have no control over their inventory so you have no way of knowing whether items are out of stock or not. You will end up having to explain the delay to your customers who will probably never come back to buy again, and repeat custom is what really drives a business forward.

Returns – You have to make sure that your drop shipper accepts returned items. If they don't, guess who'll get stuck with the cost if the customer isn't happy?

Good Drop Shippers – Finding a trustworthy and above all, reliable drop shipper is the hardest task. Avoid drop shippers that solicit your business. Contact the manufacturer of the products you would like to sell, and ask them if they provide drop shipping services. Some manufacturers do offer this service; if they don't, ask them to recommend a reputable drop shipper of their products. Look in trade magazines associated with the product line you wish to sell. Many manufacturers and distributors advertise in the back of trade magazines. There are lots of forums online about drop shipping, so subscribe to some of them and check out who's using who.

How to Choose a Drop Ship Product:

This is a basic list of the things that might help you to choose profitable products.

- If your drop ship supplier provides an exportable data file then use that data in a spreadsheet to see which items have the highest profit margins. If you aren't used to spreadsheets, try Microsoft Excel. There are lots of online tutorials that show you how to use it.

- Compare your cost to the price of the same items sold on sites like Amazon.com or on the 'Buy it Now' products on eBay.
- Compare your cost with price comparison sites such as:
  www.pricechecker.co.uk
  www.shopzilla.co.uk
  www.pricerunner.co.uk
  www.moneysupermarket.co.uk

---

**TOP TIP**

Lots of comparison sites have a 'hot list' of popular items. This might be a good place to locate possible product lines to sell, as long as you can source them cheaply enough at wholesale.

---

**Buying Wholesale**

The same rule applies to making money here as it does to drop shipping: 'buy low and sell high'. But as you won't be using a drop shipper you have to think about all the things a drop shipper would have done for you.

Buying Stock – You can't just buy one product at a time when the customer orders it, you have to buy stock, which means you have to have the money upfront. A wholesaler will offer you an account but if you are a new customer don't expect to get good credit terms. You also have to manage your stock and work out how much to buy at a time. The biggest mistake you can make is to buy a huge amount of stock and then not be able to sell it. Your capital is then tied up in a warehouse. I made this mistake once, by ordering too big a print run of some books I'd published, which didn't sell straight away. I had a warehouse full of them and an empty bank account. It very nearly wrecked my business.

Warehousing – You will need to have somewhere to store your stock. If you are selling small items of jewellery then you may be able to put them in a spare room. But if you are selling bicycles then you are going to need more space!

Getting Products to Your Customers – You are either going to have to do all of this yourself or pay someone else to do it for you. We'll talk more about this in Chapter Twenty-Two.

Returns – Not everyone will be happy with your products and they may want to send them back. You will have to work out whether you pay for the return P & P or they will (this usually varies depending on the reason for the return), and you will have to handle refunds. If you sell products that can't be sold to another customer because they're partly used, then you've lost that money.

**Selling Your Services**

You may find that *you* are your own product. You may have skills you can offer to people that they can access online, or you can use your website to market your services. Your customers could pay for your services online even if you offer those services in person. You could be an accountant, graphic artist, trainer, copy-writer, coach, or counsellor. If you have a skill then you may be able to exploit it on the net.

How profitable this is as a business model will depend on your fees, but ultimately it will also depend on how many hours there are in a day. Just as if you were offering your services offline only, you can only give your services to one client at a time, usually. You could of course employ others like you to offer the same service, and then the profit will depend on how much you pay them.

There is one way to turn this model on its head and that is to sell your service as a product. Many professionals create information products like online courses which can be downloaded. Your pour your expertise into creating the course and then it pays for itself over and over again as people buy it.

You can also offer products on your website or complementary services that go along with yours. For instance, if you are a personal trainer, you could offer your services through your website, and then sell supplements or home gym equipment and work-out clothing on your site.

There are certain things you need to succeed when selling your services online. You have to be credible. No one is going to buy work-out clothes from you if you are really overweight and look unfit. And no one is going to buy beauty products from someone who doesn't look like they take care of their appearance. You need to have the experience and the credentials to successfully sell your services and to stand out from the herd.

You can't slowly establish a rapport with a prospective client as you would in the real world because you aren't standing in front of them. So you have to convince them online that you are the right person for the job. Remember, your competitors are only a click away.

Make sure your website features all the things that make you the perfect choice for a potential customer. If you have qualifications then display them. Your 'About Us' page should let your visitors know why you are good at what you do. Display a client list, preferably with testimonials. If you don't have a client list, then get testimonials from people you have worked with in the past. Don't forget Facebook 'likes' are also testimonials, so use social media. If you have clients, get their permission to write up case studies to show your success stories. If those clients will let you, show their pictures or use video testimonials from them.

And don't forget to show off. If you have appeared in the press or on TV or radio then put your press clippings online and put a YouTube link to the program on your site.

---

**TOP TIP**

If you have any awards make sure the awards logo is prominently displayed. My company has been the winner of the ETO Best Erotic Book Brand several years running. I make sure that's prominently displayed on our site. We were also winners of the IPG (the Independent Publishers Guild) Specialist Publisher of the Year in 2013, being chosen over long-established companies such as Faber & Faber. I have added this to the signature of all company emails.

---

### Selling Information

You can find any information you want on the internet. But how long does it take you, and how reliable is the information when you find it? Some of the most successful online businesses are

ones that organise information, from Yahoo to:
www.moneysupermarket.co.uk.

Almost any information can be packaged and sold. You can either collate, organise, and compare information for a fee, or create information products from scratch, like the aforementioned downloadable online courses.

This is such a huge growth area online that there's an entire chapter on this subject; if this interests you, there's more detail in Chapter Thirteen. It's an enormous and growing field. All it requires is that you create your product, replicate it into a format that's downloadable, put it up for sale, and then keep it fresh and updated.

How much you can earn doing this is very difficult to quantify. It's a relatively new industry and it's changing all the time.

## Chapter Twelve
## Finding a Niche

As you have to compete with everyone on the web, from the tiniest shop to the biggest multi-national, it's useful to look at niches: these are small areas within a marketplace that can be very profitable.

Niche marketing means promoting a product to a specific group of people on the web who are not being catered for. Basically, you find a demand that isn't being met then you step in and provide a solution.

Niche markets can cater for almost anything. From self-help books for introverts to fancy dress costumes in plus sizes, kitchen utensils for the elderly to an e-book on five-mile walks in Cumbria.

Virtually anything you can think of could be a niche. The possibilities and potential niche markets online are vast and limitless. To find these prospects, look for answers which solve dilemmas or specific issues.

You can tap into niches by focussing on all kinds of areas, like children, baby boomers, the grey pound (pensioners), the pink pound (the gay market), self-help enthusiasts, fitness and weight loss, nutrition – the list is endless.

The best way to go about finding a niche is to think of topics you are interested in and focus on potential customers that will benefit from your product or service.

Profitable

These markets are active with people who are more than willing to pay for an answer or have a need met. No matter what niche you decide to pursue, remember you're on a level playing field with everyone else.

Your marketing message must make your niche audience feel your offering is custom-made for them. This would give them the feeling that someone cares about their needs and the vendor has found or come up with a product just for them.

## Strategy for Finding a Niche

### Brainstorm

Get a piece of paper and list all the things you're interested in. You don't have to be an expert but it helps if it's something you care about. No idea is too silly. You would be amazed what niches are not catered for. Remember, just because it's a small niche doesn't mean there's no money in it. It's highly likely there won't be much competition.

---

**Small Warning!**
Be careful of thinking you have found a niche where there is no competition at all. If no one is selling in that market it may be that there is no profit to be made. You have to know that people are hungry to pay for something. If people are searching for your niche, check that they aren't using the word 'free' in the search. That's a big clue that they don't want to pay!

---

### Mine Your Knowledge

Now write down everything you already have some kind of knowledge about. Again, you don't have to be an expert but you do need a good degree of knowledge. For instance, if you have children you certainly know something about parenting or education. If you spend your holidays in Mallorca every year then you may know something about tourism in Mallorca.

### Mine Your Experience

The next step is to write down everything where you have real experience, perhaps it's to do with your job or another area where you think you are, if not an expert, then certainly well-versed.

### Start Prioritising

Start crossing things out and highlighting the things you'd enjoy.

For instance, if you have experience of backpacking round the world as a student you might want to look for products to sell that are relevant to that market: universal bathplugs, perhaps!

# Chapter Thirteen
## Selling Information

Information products are selling fast on the internet. It's attractive to potential entrepreneurs because you 'make money while you sleep'. That is once you have created your information products, they sell over and over again.

I sell e-books. I don't create them, my authors do, but it's the same principle. Once the book is written, we edit it and produce an e-book, which doesn't need to be re-printed, and can be bought and downloaded an unlimited number of times. This involves far less risk than print books, because we don't have to invest money in physical stock which may not sell. E-books are also extremely versatile; it's easy to correct any mistakes by re-uploading the file, which of course cannot be done once books have gone to print.

Along with e-books, Accent Press also releases editions of our books in audio format, another information product that is growing in popularity and can be downloaded again and again with none of the risks of physical stock.

Once you have created your product you can ping it anywhere in the world in a download or an email.

### Creating Information Products

The information you choose to package will depend on your knowledge and expertise. Remember that a lot of the information you want to package may be freely available on the net for nothing, so you have to add value to the information. People pay for experience and know-how.

If you notice that a large number of people are having a problem with something, and the information isn't available in a usable form online, then you may have found a gap in the market. The information may be available but it may be hard to find or badly explained. Perhaps the information takes a very long time to find and you can offer it in one quick download.

Organising Information

We're all time-poor these days and life becomes much easier when other people organise information for us. Some sites make money from creating an 'edit' of information or products, like www.netaporter.co.uk. This site trawls high-end products and only stocks the ones it recommends. If you want someone to take the hard work out of searching, they've done it for you. They combine this with a product site as you can actually buy the products online. So it's a combination of information site and product site.

Other sites just offer information. Take Nigel Clarke, an IT manager and consultant. In 2013 he mapped out how to get past the infuriating telephone menus that greet you when you call almost any company these days. We all hate them and you can spend your life going through the options. He rang every company he could find and listed the options on a website www.pleasepress1.co.uk.

You can search his site to get the shortcuts to get to the person you need quickly. Now, that was an awful lot of work and the service is free. But he will be able to monetise it once it's successful. If he doesn't want to monetise it, he's certainly given his IT consultancy a huge publicity boost.

Martin Lewis is a crusading financial journalist. He made money from information when he turned his money-saving crusade into a website called www.moneysavingexpert.co.uk. He set up the website in 2003 for £100 and it sold it in 2012 for £87 million.

**E-Books**

Creating e-books is a very common way to organise and sell information. Kindle and other e-readers are becoming so common now that downloading e-books is becoming second nature to most people.

Don't think of e-books just as books though. They can take any form, from academic papers to how-to manuals with diagrams and illustrations.

Most people type up their information in Microsoft Word then save their material as a PDF file. PDFs were originally created so companies could share documents, as once a PDF is created the content can't be easily altered. So it's the natural format for e-books.

Kindle is the most popular e-reader at the time of writing, so now many authors are converting their e-books to the Kindle format so they can sell them on Amazon's Kindle store.

www.amazon.co.uk/Kindle-eBooks

Once you have created your e-books there are various ways to make money out of them. You can of course sell them directly from your website, or you can list them on iTunes or Amazon. There are also information distribution websites: www.ClickBank.com www.lulu.com www.smashwords.com

## Creating Video Products

Do you look for information on YouTube rather than Google? There are so many tutorials on YouTube, put there by users, that you can learn to do practically anything. If a subject is complicated it's often much quicker and less painful to learn from someone who is explaining something to you visually than it is wading through written information.

Many web-preneurs are taking full advantage of this trend and it doesn't show any signs of slowing down.

So how do you make money from video products if there are already free ones on the web? You will have noticed the adverts on some videos on YouTube. If you get enough viewers then YouTube shares the revenue from the ad they place with the creator of the video. It's a 70/30 split, with you getting the 30%: www.youtube.com/partners.

You can use these videos to get people to come to your site. You can create a trailer and upload it as a preview of a longer version they can buy from you. Or you can use the video to get people to buy your products or services.

You can also find a business that has an affiliate program and make a video about their product or service. When someone clicks on your video they're taken to the affiliate where they can buy that product or service. As an affiliate you get a percentage of the sale.

## Webinars

What's a webinar? you may ask. It's a seminar, on the web. So if you can teach something that needs more interaction with your clients than a video you can create webinars. You can now transmit audio, video, and text all at once.

Think of it as inviting an audience to your classroom where they can watch and listen to you, view whatever material you put up, such as a PowerPoint, and they can use a chat window to ask you questions or speak to the others who have joined the class.

This has all been made possible with fast broadband which means good simultaneous transmission. Your audience can watch or listen to you live.

But you can also record your webinars then sell them as downloads. The customers get the same information instantly, as they can download the webinar as soon as they pay. The only thing they don't get is the ability to participate. So you can sell the download more cheaply than the original webinar. As long as the information in your webinar doesn't go out of date you can sell it over and over again.

I don't do webinars but I could easily set one up for potential authors. I could do a masterclass on writing romantic fiction and invite people to pay to 'attend'. It's much easier for many people to attend an online course than it is a real world one, and it can be significantly cheaper.

To get people to sign up for your webinar you need to advertise the time and date, then charge people to attend and provide a link for your customers to access it. Make sure you pick a time and date that will be suitable for your audience. Think about when they are available, what time zone they are in, and how much time they will have to spare.

These companies offer webinar facilities to help you create and deliver your content: www.workcast.co.uk www.webex.com.

## Chapter Fourteen
## Selling on eBay

Selling on eBay is one of the quickest ways to start selling online and it also offers you the chance to dip your toe in the water of online commerce. You don't need any expertise in sales, advertising, or marketing.

EBay does your advertising and marketing for you. You can set up an eBay shop in the time it takes to drink a couple of lattes and it will only cost you the same amount as buying them in the first place.

So far so good, but eBay success takes a little more work. You have to set up your shop and your listings correctly to start making money. Every listing costs you money so you need those listings to really work for you.

Track Record

Before you can set up an eBay shop you have to be a member of the site and have a feedback score of 10. Either that or you need to be PayPal Verified, which means you need to connect your PayPal identity to a bank account.

### Building Your Shop

Don't do anything until you have your products ready to go, or you will be paying for your shop while it sits idle and empty. Or worse, if people really want your products, then you could get your first sale in hours or even minutes and you have to fulfil that sale. Your customers will expect to get their products in a couple of days at most, and if they don't get what they bought quickly they will waste no time in giving you bad feedback, which is the last thing you want.

Think about how you buy from sites like eBay. Don't you always look at the feedback first? Negative feedback will kill your business quickly so make sure you are ready to roll before you open your shop.

## Listings & Pricing

Take some time to look at similar products on eBay to see how people are listing and pricing them. You won't get far if you are selling identical items at a much higher cost. You also want your listing to look as good as possible. EBay offers all sorts of options to 'enhance' your listing but these usually add to the cost. But if you have 50 of a product to sell, you are only paying for one listing, so it may be worth your while enhancing your listing so that it stands out. Bear in mind though that selling fees apply to every sale, not every listing.

## Where to Start?

I'll assume that you have eBay membership and that you meet the requirements to set up a shop. Go to www.ebay.co.uk/shops and click 'Open Shop'. They offer different types of shop – Basic, Featured, and Anchor, at very different prices. Featured shops have lower fees but a higher monthly fee, so you need to sell a lot of products to make a profit. Featured shops will get a higher listing but you need to walk before you can run. Start with a Basic Shop.

## Naming Your Shop

We've talked about keywords that websites need to attract Google. The same applies here. Use keywords in the name of your shop. If you have a website then your shop name should be similar to your domain name.

## Managing Your Shop

You will be offered an option called 'Quick Shop Tune-up' which you can use to sort out the settings. But you can also do this manually by going to 'My eBay' then selecting 'Selling'. You will get a shortcuts menu then you can click 'Manage My Shop'.

## Design Your Shop

The display settings let you set out how you would like your shop to look. So this is where you can add your logo. Go to Chapter Eight to find out how to get a good logo.

If you have a website you should try to keep your branding consistent, so go for the same or a similar colour scheme so it doesn't look too different from your own site.

There are only a limited number of 'themes' for your eBay shop, but at least that makes design simpler and it also means that you don't have to agonise too long over making it look spectacular to beat the competition, because all eBay shops have to choose from the same themes.

When you have finished customising you shop you can preview it to check your handiwork.

## Making Money

As a newbie on eBay you aren't coming out of the starting blocks at the same point as your competitors. I'm afraid you are way back on the track and they get a head start. Why? Because eBay rewards established shops and sellers who have sold a lot of products and have good feedback. So when you start your shop on eBay you will probably appear at the bottom of the search results.

You will probably have bought stuff on eBay at some point and even if you haven't you have almost certainly bought from online shops like Amazon. So you will know that the lower down the search results a product is, the less likely you are to click on it and buy, if there are lots of products above it that are similar or the same.

## Listings

So how can you bump yourself up the search rankings? EBay are not forthcoming with information about how they rank results but they seem to favour listings that have optional extras, which makes them more expensive. They also seem to like items that offer free postage. So the canny seller incorporates the cost of the postage in the cost of the item.

Titles are important, so choose a title with impact and make sure you use a keyword. Have your listings reflect the fact that the items are 'New', as many goods on eBay are second-hand.

Pictures are very important. Why would you buy something without seeing it? The advice on using images is the same as it is for using images on your own website. Make sure they are good images and look professional. See Chapter Eight for more details.

Get your potential customer's attention, because they won't have much patience if your listing isn't straight to the point. Make sure you include your USP if you have one.

### Buy it Now or Auction

In most cases you should list your items as 'Buy it Now' rather than putting them in an auction. You want to appear as a shop to your customer, so list how many of the product you have to sell, or show that you offer it in different sizes or colours if there are options.

### Testing Your Listing

You can test the effectiveness of your listings by 'split-testing' them. This means that you create two listings for the same product and make the second one slightly different from the first, usually by just changing one feature. Once they have both finished you can compare which listing worked best. For instance, if you have a hundred items and 'Listing 1' achieves 60 sales but 'Listing 2' only achieves 20, you know that 'Listing 1' is more effective.

You could also test whether you can get higher up the rankings by offering one lot of products with free postage and the second lot with a charge.

You have to put a little work into eBay to make money and testing your listings is the best way to find what works for your products.

### More Testing

There is an option called 'Make Your Listing Stand Out'. Most of these will boost your sales, even if only slightly, so they're worth considering.

Be aware that eBay features are often expensive, so think about them carefully before you invest your money.

### Check the Final Fee

Once you have looked over your listing and you are happy with it make sure you review the Final Value Fee. This is paid per sale, not per listing. So you have to check your figures to make sure you are still making a profit once those fees are paid.

### Upload

Once you are happy with the final listing and the fees, click 'Save this listing as a template' and then you can use it for other products you want to list. Don't go looking for it immediately with search keywords as it will take a few minutes before you can do that. So go and have another latte!

## Chapter Fifteen
## Selling on Amazon

Selling on Amazon means you can see your products nestling happily alongside those of the biggest retailers in the world. Amazon is trusted by its customers and there are millions of them, so you instantly have an enormous potential customer base. And if you are new to selling they will take care of the payment processing, the warehousing, and the shipping, for a fee.

You can use Amazon in one of two ways: as your primary shop window, or as an extra avenue. If your customers would find it difficult to find you through search engines then it provides a way to get your potential customers to your virtual door. There are certain product types they don't sell but they are on a mission to be the biggest online retailer in the world. There isn't much you can't buy on Amazon any more.

### Selling Only Through Amazon

You should choose this option only if your product category is strongly associated with what Amazon sells. If you sell unique products you don't want your customers to get distracted by Amazon's 'Customers who bought this item also bought ...'

If you want to create your own e-commerce platform you can opt for Amazon's Webstore, which creates an independent shop. But be careful about relying too heavily on Amazon sales only. If they change their terms and conditions and you aren't happy with the changes, then you don't have another sales avenue.

### Shipping

One of the big advantages to selling on Amazon is that by using their fulfilment (postage, packaging, and delivery arrangements) you can sell a much wider range of products. You don't need warehousing and you don't need to worry about the efficiency of your shipping method because Amazon is used to handling a mind-boggling amount of products every day, very efficiently.

If you opt for using their Fulfilment by Amazon service then you just send them products, which Amazon then ship when they're ordered. All you have to do is to send more products as required.

Of course, they don't do this for free, they are a business. So your margin on each product will be smaller, but it does free up your time to work on your business and not in your business. While they're shipping your products you can spend your time promoting them.

### Setting up an Amazon Shop

One of the major plus points of setting up an Amazon shop is that it is relatively quick. But you do have to make a decision up front about how much stock you think you are likely to sell. Amazon asks you from the outset whether you will sell a small amount or a lot. How do you decide what a lot is? Well, the trigger point is more than 33 items a month. Let me explain:

### Standard versus Pro Merchant Account

The Standard merchant account charges per item on top of the normal seller fees which you pay on completion of a sale. This is what Amazon says:

*Individuals selling at Marketplace pay a GBP 0.86 per item completion fee, plus a closing fee that is a percentage of the sales price for each item sold based on the product type.*

If you sign up for a Pro Merchant account then you will be charged a flat rate of £25 a month plus VAT.

So if you sell more than 33 items it is cheaper to be a Pro Merchant and pay a monthly flat rate.

### Pro Merchant

If you are nervous about committing to a flat fee as you aren't sure you can make enough sales then you can always start with a standard account and upgrade when your business grows.

But if you are selling something unusual that is not in Amazon's database then you will need a Pro Merchant account. Only Pro Merchants are allowed to add products not in the database. This gives you an advantage as there will be fewer people selling that product.

## Getting Started

You probably already have an Amazon account, you may have started off like many, buying books, and now buy a host of other things. You can use the same login to set up your merchant account, but I am a firm believer in keeping business and personal life separate, so I would set up a different login. It will take a little longer, a few days, while they verify you, but it's better to wait a few days and get it right.

## Getting Your Settings Right

Once you are all signed up you will be able to alter your shop's settings in the Seller Central control panel. Make sure you set this up very carefully, especially the shipping settings. If you are selling certain standard items like CDs or DVDs then standard postal costs are made by Amazon. But if you sell anything else the cost of the postage and shipping is up to you.

| **TOP TIP** |
|---|
| Don't be tempted to pluck a figure out of the air, or make an 'educated' guess. If you get your postage figures wrong, you will be haemorrhaging money every time you make a sale. |

Price your shipping based on weight as that's what it will actually cost you. The exact cost will depend on your shipping method, but take some time to get this right.

## Adding Your Products

Like on eBay, you will have to place your products in to categories. So spend some time looking at which categories your competitors have chosen for their products and use those. Adding the products is straightforward with an Inventory/Add Product option. If you are adding a new product then click 'Create New Product'. Amazon make it pretty straightforward.

On the Information page you will notice that some fields are mandatory and some optional. Fill in as much as you possibly can if you want to stand out from the competition. The more you tell your potential customers the more likely they are to become actual customers. I'll go through the fields quickly here:

### Barcodes

You will see that many categories include a mandatory request for a barcode. You'll see a field on the form asking for 'EAN or UPC'. EAN is the numbering format for Europe.

Don't panic if your products don't have barcodes as that's simple to remedy. Many companies now buy these barcodes in bulk and sell them on.

### Do I need a Barcode?

If you are storing and despatching the products yourself, you don't need to put the barcode image on to your product, but you can if you want to. If, however, you are using Amazon's fulfilment service then you should put the barcode image on to your product.

See companies like Get-A-Barcode for barcode services.

### Pricing

After you have filled in the product information you will be taken to the 'Offer' page. Again, put as much information in it as you can. Amazon gives you the option to discount for a fixed period, which is a good idea as it makes you stand out from the competition and gets your business going. This is ideal if you are selling a product which will have your customers coming back for repeat business.

### Images

As with adding images to your own website, add as many as you can to help the customer get a real feel for the product. This is especially true if the product has lots of features which you can show off in the images.

## Description

It's very important to get the 'Key Product Features' right. You may have noticed when you buy something that there is a section with a list on a product showing the Technical Details. This is where your key product features will show up. Spend time on the Product Description Field. It's very easy when you know your products inside out to forget to describe them properly. Imagine what it's like for a customer who doesn't know anything about them, and start from there. You can format the text so that your description can appear as a list, and use bold or italics and paragraphs. Use these! Otherwise the description will just be one big blob of a paragraph which won't grab anyone's attention unless they are determined to read it. Make the benefits *stand out from the rest!*

---
**TOP TIP**
Under Search Terms, don't put the product name or manufacturer as Amazon will do that automatically. Use *your* keywords.

---

## More Details

This field isn't mandatory but if you have chosen to price your shipping by weight you must put that here.

Once you have hit Save and Finish, wait a few minutes for Amazon to upload everything then check your listing.

## Customers

Before you pat yourself on the back thinking 'that was easy', remember that putting up an Amazon shop may be relatively simple, but you still have to sell the products. Just like any other business you have find your customers, convince them to buy your products, and then get the products to them in perfect condition, quickly, and efficiently.

If you have a bricks-and-mortar shop then, assuming you have a reasonable location, you will have 'footfall': people will be physically walking past your shop, so some of them will find you by accident and come in.

With online shops and therefore with Amazon shops, they have to be attracted because they won't just be wandering past. So let's assume you have done all the right things, you have put your products in and chosen the right categories and great keywords. Most products are sold because someone searched for them on Amazon or Google, so the higher up the rankings you come, the better your chances.

## Search Terms

As with all searches online, the terms used will determine what gets thrown up. So I am going to talk about keywords again. It's really important to get your keywords right. They have to be in the product title but you can add more or variations of them in the section called 'Search Terms' where you enter your product details.

Good keywords could mean the difference between dominating in a category or not appearing at all after a search.

## Chapter Sixteen
## Blog for Profit

Bridget Jones could have made a fortune with a blog if she'd been real. Blogs started out as online diaries and observations on life, but now you can make money from them. Companies and individuals have adopted blogging as a way to sell products and services, and some bloggers just create an enormous following and monetise that.

It's easy for a novice to blog; you don't have to be a web designer. Programs like www.WordPress.com and Google's www.Blogger.com make it easy to get up and running and they're free.

WordPress is now probably the most popular blogging tool – my company loves it! You can start with the hosted version and upgrade to a self-hosted version later at www.wordpress.org. This means you can grow your blog into a business without having to move your site. A WordPress blog can also be your entire site and not just a blog. It's a very powerful tool.

**So how do you make money with a blog?**

Well, the key is to write something people want to read. Good blogs are full of constantly updated content, unlike websites which rarely change. The internet allows us all to communicate instantly. You don't have to wait a month for your favourite beauty magazine to come out with hints and tips on the latest products. Find a great beauty blogger and you can get the information immediately. Want to know what the best eczema cream is for your baby? Find a blogger who's tested them all.

---

**TOP TIP**
The more often you blog, the higher your ranking will be in Google. Google loves changing content. And the best time to post

is early in the morning. That's because there's a good chance your content will be picked up by news sites and other bloggers. That means you will get more links to your site and more referrals.

BEWARE!

Don't set up a blog and then abandon it or hardly update it. That will just annoy people who have decided to follow you. Blogging only works if you keep it fresh.

### What Shall I Write About?

Well, that depends on your expertise and your interests. You can choose to write on a specific trend or market, or you could write a more personal blog. Do choose a topic that has an audience, whether it's a solid niche one or a wide audience. That's the only way you will make money.

### How Should I Write?

You must establish your tone of voice. Your readers need a sense of who you are and how you think. The tone of blogs is usually quite chatty and informal. Let your readers get to know you and how you think. Although there's no reason you can't have guest bloggers on your site if it is interesting to your audience. If you run a company and more than one person is maintaining the blog, make sure you all have the same idea of how it should sound and what it should contain. You want everyone singing off the same hymn sheet.

### Blog Posts

You don't have to write *War and Peace* every time you post. A blog entry might just be a few lines, or it could be the equivalent of an article, 500 words or more. Visitors can tell how often you blog as each posting is dated with a time and date stamp.

Here are some examples of types of post.

Links to Something Interesting – If you see something your readers will be interested in, let them know with a few short sentences and then give them the link. If you have written a previous blog post on the subject you can also provide a link to that.

Current Affairs – You can discuss topical issues or things that crop up in the news or in your marketplace. It could be about absolutely anything from news to sport, celebrities to special events. If people are discussing something, they may be searching for information about it. So if you have blogged about it, you may come up in their Google search.

Find Tie-ins – Don't be afraid to comment on something that isn't directly related to what you write about. If a celebrity is trying to lose weight and you write a diet blog then write about that celeb's battle with the pounds.

Evergreen content – This is what timeless content is known as. It describes the kind of stories that are always of interest to readers. For example, a fitness magazine will run a story about abdominal workouts or a beauty magazine will run an article on how to choose a foundation. You can find those articles at any time because they are general and not pegged to an event.

## Sell the Content

Many bloggers have made money by taking their best content, repackaging it, and selling it as an information product or e-book. You may think 'but the info is available free why would they buy?' You don't have to charge very much, maybe £1.99. You are saving the people the trouble of searching your blog, and anything that saves people time is worth money. And if it gets downloaded thousands of times then the money adds up quickly. You could also turn your best information into a series of videos on YouTube and get advertising on your very own channel.

## AdSense

You are probably familiar with AdWords, these are the adverts on the right-hand side of a Google search page. As a business you might pay for AdWords to promote your business. Well this is the other side of the coin. This is where people pay to put ads on your site.

The most popular types are links that complement the topic you write about. These are called contextual ads. Google looks for content that matches the ads and pairs them up. You don't have to do any selling. It works well because the adverts are directly relevant to your blog and of interest to your readership.

The ads usually show up on the sidebar of your site but you can place them through your site. My advice is: don't put them where they will get in the way of the content. That will annoy your readership and you have worked too hard to build up a loyal following.

To add AdSense go to Google and click the Get Started with AdSense button, and it's very straightforward from there: accounts.google.com/getstartedadsense

You have to identify keywords that Google will use to match the ads to your content, so make sure you use the right keywords, things that will bring people who want to buy from your advertisers to your blog.

### Sell from Your Blog

As well as informing your readership, you can sell to them too. You will in all likelihood want to sell products that relate to your content, especially if you have recommended them. You can either sell from your blog directly or you could join an affiliate scheme. This is a scheme where you partner with another vendor who runs affiliates. You put a link to the product they sell on your site, when your visitor clicks through the link to your affiliate and buys the product from them, you get a percentage.

### Cost

Blogging has very low overheads. If you already have a website, talk to your hosting company to see whether they can integrate a blog into your existing website. If you do this, your blogging audience will then see your other offerings which may be an online store or a website selling your services.

## Chapter Seventeen
## Making Money from Videos

We've all seen YouTube. What started as a place for USG or User Generated Content, put on the site for fun, is now a site awash with people monetising their content. There are many success stories of people who have made money by uploading their videos, but it is getting harder. The good thing is that YouTube *does* want people to make money on the site.

In April 2013 YouTube launched a new revenue-sharing program. Before this, creators had to pair sponsors' ads with their videos and get YouTube's permission. Now it's all been automated with a 'monetize' button. If you create videos you get about half the advertising proceeds. YouTube usually finds the advertisers, although you can approach sponsors directly.

> *'If they can generate an audience, they can start making money.'*
> Tom Pickett, YouTube Vice President, Global Operations.

We've all seen what a smash hit Korean pop star Psy has been with 'Gangnam Style'.
www.youtube.com/gangnamstyle
Hit videos go viral at breathtaking speed, and that's the goal of every wannabe YouTube entrepreneur and professional advertiser on the site. If your video gets enough hits, then you can get money.

Here are some big numbers for you:
- 1 billion people visit the site every month
- Advertisers paid an estimated $4 billion for YouTube ads in 2012 – that's up 60 percent from 2011

Now before you go rushing for the video camera let me tell you that around a million people have signed up for this revenue-sharing program and they have been rather disappointed with the returns. Why might that be?

Here are some more big numbers for you.

At the time of writing this …

- 72 hours of content is uploaded every minute.
- This is up from 2011 when it was 48 hours a minute

Also the rates that advertisers pay to be on popular videos have fallen by about 30 per cent since 2012.

## Can I Make it Work?

Most of what's on YouTube is not what advertisers want, so you have to create quality content.

If you need help to create content there are networks that take a cut for helping clients with production costs, getting paid sponsorships, or securing higher ad rates by selling ads directly to marketers instead of relying on YouTube.

One of the biggest networks is www.machinima.com which is part backed by Google and has over 6,000 creators. It specialises in videos for male gamers aged 18-34. It negotiates ad rates directly with sponsors, often at a premium because it has a good audience.

You don't have to sign up with a big network, however. You just have to find a way to drive traffic to your channel, and all the marketing strategies in this book apply to that. If you can find a way to provide videos that people want to watch in large numbers then you have the opportunity to make money.

You can make money if you are a professional filmmaker or just make hobby videos. They key is getting people to watch your videos and share them with their friends.

### Instruction videos

You don't need an instruction manual on anything any more, because someone, somewhere, will have made a video instruction manual and you will find it on YouTube. You can even find video tutorials on YouTube telling you … how to make money on YouTube!

This can be anything from corporate-style training videos to make-up tutorials. A good example is www.pixiwoo.com. This is a make-up tutorial site set up by two sisters. They now have their own channel and over 500 videos. They also run real-world courses in their Norwich make-up studio. So the site is fantastic advertising for their bricks-and-mortar business and also makes them money. They also have very good make-up advice!

## Haulers

Shopping haulers are people who buy things then record their reviews. This started as a trend among teenage girls who vlogged – that is they video blogged. It's basically showing off your shopping and telling your 'friends'.

Here are some tips on being successful on YouTube:

- Do something original – Copying someone else, unless you do it so much better, is not going to get you noticed. You might make a small amount of money if you're on a popular trend, but it will be short-lived. Remember all those copies of Gangnam Style and the Harlem Shake that rocketed around YouTube? If you haven't seen them, just go online, there were so many.
- You have 15 seconds – That's when you need to grab people's attention. People have no patience, you have to grab them quickly if you want to keep them watching and share with their friends.
- Make More Videos – You can be a huge hit with one video but to make real money you need to get people coming back to you to see your latest offering, you need subscribers. Plan a series, not a one-hit wonder. Remember www.pixiwoo.com? They have 500 videos.

## Chapter Eighteen
## Affiliate Programs

Affiliate programs are basically revenue-sharing plans. You find a company that sells products or services and runs an affiliate scheme. You join the scheme, then put links to that company's products on your website. When someone clicks through to their site and buys something, you get a small percentage of the profit. The products can be physical goods, services, downloads, webinars, or pretty much anything you can sell online.

Some affiliate programs are good, some are downright awful, so I'll try and help you sort the wheat from the chaff so you can start earning money!

### How the Programs Work

It's ridiculously easy to set one of these up. But there will only be money if you have good traffic to your website that are hungry to buy and you have chosen the right affiliate program.

I would recommend finding a product or service that you really like and is a quality product. People do make money with shoddy products, but at the end of the day it's *your* reputation. People won't come back to you if they find one of your recommendations is shabby. You want to keep your readership so go for the good stuff. It's also much easier to sell and recommend something you like and believe in.

### How Do I Find An Affiliate Program?

Let's look at the different types of program and where you will find them.

'A List' Affiliate Networks

This just means a trusted and well-recognised program.

Typically they are large and often have secure relationships with the biggest brands. So if you want to plug a household brand name you are likely to find the program being run through an A List network like these.

- Commission Junction
- Linkshare
- Shareasale

These are big0name companies with a long standing history and offer management to companies who otherwise wouldn't know what they're doing. But unless you are a huge affiliate you are unlikely to get much attention from them. They also take longer to pay than smaller programs. They can command larger fees and commissions from their merchants which can mean there's less money left over for you.

### E-Product Networks

These are networks that offer electronic downloadable products like e-books.

- Clickbank
- E-Junkie
- Avangate (software products)

One of the bigger issues with using these types of network is that they are filled with terrible products and only a few really good ones. You really have no way of knowing which products are any good until you review them yourself. That can become rather expensive.

### Secondary Affiliate Networks

These are smaller versions of the A-List networks, usually with smaller brands and very often lower-quality brands. Some of them have a reputation for always paying and standing by the affiliate in cases where merchants try and pull some dodgy deals, but many disappear almost as quickly as they appeared in the first place. But when they do pay, they often pay more frequently and offer more methods of payment than the A-List companies. They also tend to charge smaller fees to the merchants which means there's likely to be more money for affiliates. So treat them with caution and look for reviews from other affiliates to see what their experience is.

### Independent Affiliate Programs

These are run in-house by a company that uses affiliate software. Accent Press uses a called clixGalore, which can be a great source of revenue. (The good thing from an affiliate standpoint is that because they aren't paying commissions to a middle-man, the payouts are often better. But the program needs to be managed by someone who knows what they're doing. If you go down this route, check when payments are made to make sure they are regular and scheduled. Very often independent programs are run by people who have a keen eye on their business so they look after their affiliates because it's in their interest to do so. But if the program isn't a big earner for them, they won't really focus on it, or you. They can be difficult to find, you just have to do a lot of searching, or look for products you would like to recommend and see who sells them and if they have an affiliate program.

### Search the Competition

If you read blogs or visit sites that are similar to yours, then see who they are affiliated with. See what others are recommending.

### Before You Sign Up

Always check that the contracts and payment methods are acceptable to you, as not all affiliate programs operate the same way. Look out for the following:

Commission Structure – This is usually calculated as a percentage of sales. But the amounts may be based on a minimum sales level. Some programs will pay more the more you sell. If you are selling a subscription you may get a one-off fee rather than ongoing payments.

Method of Payment – Check the currency you will be paid in

and whether you get paid monthly or quarterly. If you can choose how you get paid, get the money paid directly into your bank account.

Tracking – The affiliate program must have a record of efficient tracking or they won't know how many people have clicked through from your site. If they don't know that, they can't pay you what you're owed.

Cookies – People don't usually buy on the first click. They may look the first time, then go and have a cup of coffee and a think. They may come back half an hour later or a week later. Then they might buy. But the second time they visit they might go straight to the company's site and not go through your link. A cookie monitors where the visitor came from. So if there are cookies on the site, they can trace that person back to your original clickthrough and you get paid.

Refunds – This is very important. You need to know if, how, and when that money will be taken out of your account.

Terms and Conditions – Read them carefully. You don't want to end up being penalised or barred because you didn't follow their guidelines or had another affiliate program on your site that wasn't compatible under their T&Cs. They may also have strict marketing strategies that stop you from using certain strategies of your own.

Marketing Tools – Affiliate programs usually have their own which help you. But make sure they are acceptable to you and find out if you are allowed to use your own.

---

**TOP TIP**

Always check out affiliate programs on forums and review sites. You don't want to find you have signed up with a dodgy company. Use the Better Business Bureau Online to see if the company has been blacklisted: http://mbc.bbb.org/. You can find out who runs the website from the look-up site http://www.whois.net/.

---

**Spotting a Dodgy Company**

- Here's a list of things that should set alarm bells ringing about an affiliate program.

- There's no money-back guarantee or product guarantees.
- Returns and refunds are difficult and complicated.
- You can't easily find their corporate information and they won't point you to it or send you any.
- You find reviews from disgruntled affiliates and customers.
- They don't offer any support for their affiliates.
- They want a sign-up fee. It should be free.

# Section Four

# Selling, Shipping and Taking Payments

## Chapter Nineteen
## How to Take Payment

Whatever your chosen method of making money on the web, you have to get paid. Making a sale is all very well, but you have to get people through the checkout so that their money goes into your bank account. So if you want to take payments online you need to work out how you are going to do that. Whichever method you decide it has to be 100% reliable and secure. The last thing you want is customers complaining that your shopping cart doesn't work, or that payments don't go through properly, or God forbid that your customers' details are hacked and stolen.

There are simple options such as sites like PayPal which sort it all for you, or you can operate a Merchant Account.

### PayPal

If you are a new business then PayPal is a very attractive option as it is relatively quick and easy. It may be your only choice as getting a merchant account may be tricky or overly expensive for a new business.

You need a verified business account, which you will link to PayPal. Customers will be redirected to PayPal's site to make their payment. If they don't have a PayPal account they can pay with their debit or credit card.

Once they've paid they go back to the order confirmation screen on your website. PayPal talks to your e-commerce software to tell it that payment has gone through and you can go ahead and ship the customer's order.

The money sits in PayPal's account until you transfer it to your bank account.

Accent Press use a standard PayPal account for processing our payments and we find it works really well for our set-up.

**PayPal Web Payments Pro**

You may find that some customers are put off when re-directed to PayPal's site and you may lose a sale. If this is a worry for you, then you can opt for PayPal Web Payments Pro. This program integrates with your site. The customer pays with their plastic card and they never see the PayPal logo. They will see the normal payment fields asking for card number and name. There is of course a charge for this service, around £20 a month on top of the transaction fee. So this will cost you more than the standard account but it may increase your conversion rate. If your customers don't have a PayPal account, they may be put off when re-directed to a heavily branded site that isn't yours.

### When Should I Upgrade?

If you want to know when it would be sensible to upgrade to Payments Pro, PayPal suggest a trigger point of over £1,000 in online payments a month.

### Is it Simple to Upgrade?

I'm afraid it's not as simple to open a Payments Pro account as a standard one because PayPal are more exposed to chargebacks. If you are a new company PayPal will probably cover themselves by keeping a reserve of the money they take for 90 days. So they will hold back a percentage of the takings and you get them 90 days later. This could gum up your cash flow when you start, but remember that if you are making sales every day then you get money back in a trickle every day after the 90 days.

### Google Checkout

Google Checkout is very similar to PWPS. Your customer needs a Google Checkout account. More and more people are signing up for one, and you will know if you have an android phone, you sign up to pay for apps. But it would be silly to rely on this alone; you can never run a successful business if you only use Google Checkout.

PWPS holds on to a reserve if you are a new business. Google Checkout holds on to the lot. For the first 60 days after you sign up you will have to wait 10 days to get paid from a sale. This is their probationary period. After that you will get paid within a few days.

## Amazon Payments

One of the big plus points of using Amazon Payments is that your customers can use their Amazon accounts to pay. The checkout system is integrated into your online shop. They either finish the transaction on your site or use an Amazon pop-up window. The window isn't as distracting as the PayPal version which re-directs you to their site.

---

### WARNING
You must check that whatever e-commerce package you are using supports Amazon Payments, as not all of them do.

---

Once you've signed up for this, Amazon makes payments to you every 14 days. They also hang onto a reserve in case there are a lot of requests for refunds.

The formula for calculating the reserve is pretty complicated. They hang on to the amount of transaction disputes plus the last 14 days of sales. After six months they will replace the reserve with one based on your refund rate, which should be low if you are running your business well and you are selling good products.

## Merchant Account

Around 60% of customers in an online shop will want to pay by debit or credit card. So to take their payments you will need a merchant account and a payment gateway.

The merchant account is a type of bank account used to handle the card transactions. The gateway captures the card details so that the funds can be transferred to you, the seller.

This means you will be charged two fees for each transaction.

For example, you may have seen CardNet when you are shopping online. This is Lloyds TSB's merchant account provider. You might also have seen SagePay, which is its recommended payment gateway. CardNet will charge a percentage for each credit card payment. The rate will depend on how long you have been trading and what type of business you have. SagePay will charge £20 a month for up to 1,000 payments a quarter.

It's very difficult to get a merchant account if you are a new business. This is because when things go wrong it's the bank that has to pick up the tab. If a card is used fraudulently or not processed properly, then Visa or Mastercard will ask for a 'chargeback' from the bank which it will pass on to you. If you can't pay, the bank has to.

### How Do I Choose?

However you start, your ultimate aim should be to have a merchant account. To get a good rate you will need to show that you have been trading successfully for around two years. The cash flow implications of companies hanging on to 20% of your income could be a deciding factor, as bad cash flow can sink a new business. Around 60% of online customers pay by card. So if you only offer PWPS, then a lot of your cash is going to be tied up in the reserve. So calculate what your choice of payment method will do to your cash flow.

# Chapter Twenty
## Shopping Carts

Before you can choose a shopping cart for your website you need to understand the types of carts and their costs and features.

Customised sophisticated shopping carts with lots of items in the catalogue will not be cheap. They have to be installed, set up, customised, and tested, then connected to the payment gateway.

Carts vary from very simple manual checkouts with no pictures to sophisticated layouts that match the look of your website.

Shopping cart services which charge a monthly fee and require you to update can be very sophisticated, but take a lot of work and can be expensive if you have frequent changes.

Don't forget you are dealing with serious security, liability, and privacy law compliance issues.

Hosting companies don't usually offer tech support for your shopping cart, and you are responsible for all security. Some hackers target shopping carts and put scripts on them to also capture the credit card data that your customer is entering.

You need a good web development and maintenance company to help you monitor security issues.

When choosing the type of shopping cart you want, like all your website and internet marketing, the choices are dictated by your budget, your requirements, your marketing plan, and the image you want. Is it important to look sophisticated like a 'real business' and to offer options on multiple items? Do you need pictures of items and nice descriptions with links? Do you need it to be consistent with the look and feel of your website?

## How Do I Choose?

Think about what will be important to your customers and try to imagine the experience from their point of view. Does the cart help them process their orders quickly or does it leave them frustrated, so they click away before completing their order, losing you a sale?

Here are some features to consider.

- Save Settings – Can they leave their purchases in the shopping cart and go back to shopping to complete the purchase later?
- Product Views – Can your customers see what they're buying?
- Store Data – Entering your data can be really tedious when you are shopping online. Some customers don't want to risk their security by saving data, but some customers like to open an account and store their details with you, so they don't have to keep re-entering it.
- View Order – Most customers want to see everything in one place. When they place an order they want to see the shipping costs and all the details. They don't want to have to look at a series of pages.
- Other Considerations.
- Poor Performance – If your shopping cart doesn't work, you can't take payments. If you can't take payments your business is losing money, so this is really important.
- Support – Check you get good support with your shopping cart and find out whether this costs you extra.
- Flexibility – You may only have one type of customer now, but you may want to sell to wholesalers in the future or start an affiliate scheme, so think about your ability to grow and make sure your cart could handle it.
- Integration – Does your cart talk to your accounting software? If these two don't integrate then you will have a lot more work on your hands.

### Special Features

A good shopping cart can help you with sales and marketing. Certain extra functions could really help your bottom line.

- Bundles – If you can offer a discounted bundle of items as opposed to buying separately you might sell more.
- Coupons and Discounts – Does your cart offer the option to put in promotional codes, discounts, gift certificates, etc.?
- Free shipping – Does your cart offer free shipping if your

customer spends over a certain amount?
- Tell a Friend – Can customers pass on product pages to friends, or tell people what they've bought? Our site offers you the chance to tell Facebook what you've just purchased.

## Hosted Shopping Carts

You can opt for a third-party option, where your cart is hosted on another server and you pay for access to it. The advantage of this is that it's affordable, especially for a new business. They're simple and easy to integrate into your website. You get access to technical support and it's usually around the clock. They're also pretty flexible as you can try before you buy, and you can usually get a monthly plan to try it out.

www.goecart.com is one hosted solution that works very well.

This software works just as well for huge companies as it does for little start-ups. For small businesses they give you two options, professional or premier. Which one you choose would depend on your requirements for storage and bandwidth. The premier version offers more features, but you can choose the professional version and pay to add some extra features if you need them. The price depends on what you need and you would have to speak to a salesperson to get a quote. Don't forget to haggle. You may be able to get reductions on certain things!

## Buying Ready-Made Software

This allows you to add the software yourself to your own server. When you use this type of shopping cart, you aren't tied to a particular web host, which can be an advantage. If you end up moving providers your shopping cart isn't compromised as you are managing it yourself.

This type of shopping cart can be bought or licensed. So you have to decide if you want to pay up front to own it, or to lease it.. Check if technical support comes as part of the package as it may be an added cost.

Companies that sell off-the-shelf shopping carts include www.volusion.com and www.shopsite.com but there are many more.

## Custom Made

This is the most expensive option. There is an advantage to custom-made shopping carts in that you can get them programed exactly the way you want it – if you decide that none of the existing solutions meets your needs then you can pay to have a cart designed for your website.

But be certain you need this. Hosted and off-the-shelf carts are so good that you really would need to have very specific needs to go to the expense and trouble of having one built.

The downside of this option is that it can get really pricey; the more features and customisation you want the more work it will be for the programmer. And every time you get a problem and find something that needs changing you have to go back to them to do more work.

Shop around for a good developer. Get lots of quotes to make sure you understand what is being offered and what isn't in the package. Make sure you get the bid you choose in writing. When asking for bids send the same list of requirements to all of the companies.

Make sure you talk about support; find out if it's ongoing support and how quickly issues will be resolved. You don't want to hire someone and then find out too late that there is no support at weekends and that most of your customers buy on Saturday afternoons.

Also, make sure you know what timescale they are working to and get a definite delivery date.

# Chapter Twenty-One
## Choosing and Pricing Stock

If you have decided to sell products or downloads as opposed to services, then you need to decide what to sell and how to price it. This is especially true of physical products as you will probably want to sell a range.

When you are trying to decide on what stock to buy you have to bear in mind three things:

- Availability – Will you be able to buy the products easily and consistently? If one supplier goes out of business, will you be able to source the goods elsewhere at the right price?
- Price – Can you charge a price that will make you a profit but also be attractive to your customers? Can you find that sweet spot where people buy and you still make money?
- Range – Is there enough choice in the range to be attractive? This may not apply to you, for instance if you have one killer product that everybody wants then you may not need a range. But this is unusual.

Knowing how to choose your products can be a daunting task. So here are some tips to help you ponder.

- Familiarity – Do you know about these products already or will you have to learn about them? You need to understand what you are selling before you can really 'sell' it.
- Volume – How much does a supplier require you to buy to get a good price? Usually the more you buy the better the deal you get. But this only works in your favour if you can buy in bulk. You have to be certain you can shift the stock if you are going to be bulk ordering. You don't want your capital tied up in stock in a warehouse not making you money – remember my situation when I over-ordered on books!
- Storage – If you are buying in bulk, do you have somewhere suitable to store it or will you have to rent warehousing?

- No Storage – If you don't have money for warehousing, could you stock smaller products, or sell virtual products like e-books or software that take up little or no space?
- Size, Fragility, and Shipping – How difficult will it be to ship your products? If they are fragile, what implication does that have for the cost of shipping? The same goes for large products; it will be more expensive to get them to your customer.
- Custom-Built – If the goods are built to order, how long will the process take? If your business really takes off, you will have to keep up with demand, so do you have the skills and manpower to do that, and if not, can you get them?

### Pricing Your Products

It doesn't matter how in demand your products are, if you don't price them correctly they won't sell. So it's really important to have the right pricing strategy. If you price too high you can always bring your prices down. But what if you find you have priced too low and you could be making more money? It's much harder to put your prices up.

When deciding on price look at these factors:
- Competition – Always, always, always check out the competition. Find out who your competitors are, how many there are, and what prices they are selling at.
- Cost – You can't make money if you sell so cheaply that you can't meet your running business costs. Make sure you have taken those costs into account when you work out how much it costs you to buy a single product.
- Profit – How much of a margin do you want to make in order to make your business viable?
- Demand – There's no point having a super-duper shiny new product if no one wants to buy it. Just because you think it's fabulous doesn't mean everyone else will. Steve Jobs at Apple managed to create things and then made people want them later, but he was an exception.

Finding the right price can be really confusing, by the time you look at all the competition and pricing models your head will be hurting.

The most important thing to think about is the actual cost of your products in relation to your business. As long as you are bringing more in than is going out, you are making a profit. How much profit will depend on your skill and the market.

You can either opt for a Cost Plus Option – which means you are charging the lowest price you can get away with while making a profit. Or you can opt for the Value-Based Option – which means you are selling at the highest amount you think the customer will pay. You really have to find a way of adding value if you are going for the latter. But you may be able to do that. If you are selling something like skincare, are you in a position to offer advice along with those products? If you are selling a service, are you offering your customers a follow-up call? There are endless ways to add value so that you can charge more.

### Inventory

We have all got used to being able to buy almost anything online. This means shoppers are now very savvy and know that if a site isn't offering them what they want instantly, then another shop will, and it will be just a click away.

You have to make sure that your inventory reflects what your potential customer is looking for. This doesn't mean having thousands of items of stock, it means having the right stock.

### Competing on Price

If you have decided to compete on price then remember that your customers are looking for bargains. So you may have to change what you offer quite regularly, or provide a very wide range. It's a good idea to incorporate an 'If you liked that, you might like this …' option on your site or a 'Customers who bought that also bought …'. It showcases different options to your customers by bringing up other choices alongside the one they have chosen to view.

It may also be a good idea to refresh the offering regularly. You could have a different featured product each week so that there is a reason for your customers to come back and look.

When you start your business you will almost certainly find that stocking the right products and finding out what sells is difficult. You have to keep a close eye on what people are looking at, what's selling, and most importantly, what's not selling. It will be trial and error.

Track your results to find out what your inventory needs. Once you have worked out what visitors are looking at and buying, you can scale down what you stock.

### Specialisation

Not every business needs to sell a huge inventory. You may sell single-estate tea, or spare parts for a particular make of car. If you are focussing on being a specialist retailer, then focus on the uniqueness of your products and your offer, rather than quantity and variety. Make sure your customers know you are an expert and that it's worth their while coming to you.

---
**TOP TIP**

If a product does well and you run out, don't put 'out of stock' on the page. This makes it look like you can't run your business.

Instead put 'sold out!' This creates the impression that it's a great product that everyone wants. Make sure your customers can see that they can still order it and they will get it soon.

---

## Chapter Twenty-Two
## Fulfilling Your Orders

**So** you've built your website and customers want to buy what you're selling. Hooray! You're over a major hurdle. But now you have to get the customer's order sent out to them, in perfect condition and quickly. This is described in business as 'fulfilment'. If you are in a bricks-and-mortar shop then it's easy. The customer pays, you put the product in a bag, and off they go. But online, it's much more complicated.

From the moment the customer presses the 'Complete Your Order' button, you are on the clock. They buy online all the time and they use shops that ship things out double-quick. So you have to get this part of your business right, because if you don't, that customer won't come back, and repeat business is an essential part of making a profit.

Before you start looking for shipping companies think about your business from start to finish. You have to map out how fulfilment fits into your workflow.

Ask yourself these questions:
- If you have employees, do any of them need access to the payment and shipping system?
- Do you have a physical shop as well? If you do, then how will that tie in with your online store?
- Do you want to handle the shipping, or do you want to outsource it so that you can spend your time on other things in your business.
- When do you get the products from your supplier?
- Do you have to do anything to the product before you can sell it?
- Where are you storing it, at your own facility or somewhere else?
- How and by whom will the product be packed?

- How will you be shipping it, and how will it get from storage to shipping?

## Logistics

You need to think through these points so that you can work out the logistics of delivering your products, i.e. how you manage your operation.

There are a variety of options, but whatever you choose to do, it must work for your business.

---

**TOP TIP**

Bear in mind that if you take on many of these tasks, it may save you money in the short term, but it will mean you are working *in* your business and not *on* your business. Would your time be better spent marketing or networking?

---

## In-House

If you are just starting out then you will probably decide to do the fulfilment yourself, unless of course you are selling huge items like washing machines or cars.

Doing this does allow you to control the process, you know exactly how you want things packed and you can make sure the customer gets what they were expecting.

To start with, make sure you have enough inventory to fulfil initial orders. As you go along you will learn how much stock you need to keep.

## Suppliers

Some suppliers may want to send you batches of items so you will need to store them. But you may be able to find a supplier who operates the way supermarkets do and will supply you 'just-in-time'. This means you need less space. But you must have a reliable supplier. If they're late, then you are late sending out to your customer too.

## Storage

If you have to get outside storage, such as renting a warehouse, it's a good idea to see if the management will accept deliveries for you and allow them into that warehouse. It means you don't have to be there every time there's a delivery.

## Packing

When you start your business you will probably find that you can manage the packing yourself. But if you are successful and the business grows you may find you are spending all day packing, which is not going to help your business in the long run. So you may at this point consider either outsourcing the fulfilment or hiring someone to do the packing.

## Outsourcing

Many entrepreneurs choose to outsource their shipping as it eliminates a major headache in logistics. It also gives you a chance to spend more time on marketing, sourcing products, and networking for your business.

And who wants to spend their life packing things when they'd rather be selling them?

Luckily there are fulfilment houses that do nothing but ship orders for other companies. This means that you can find a fast, efficient company to take care of all of this for you.

Some of course are better than others, and the better they are, the more expensive they are. So you will have to do some research. But the adage 'you get what you pay for' really applies here. It's crucial that your customers get their goods in pristine condition and on time, so look at the quality and price of the service you are being offered.

What do the companies offer? This varies. Here's a list of what they may offer you.

- Reporting – You need to keep track of your orders and look at the data. So you need a company that has reporting capability you can access online so they can deliver reports to you about how many orders go out for each product.
- Customer Service – Customers will call sometimes to ask a

question about their order or to return a product and ask for a refund. So who is going to handle that call, you or the fulfilment company? Many companies have customer service teams to deal with these calls. It takes the worry out of hiring, training, and maintaining the calls. But bear in mind, if a customer starts asking questions about the products, those staff may not be able to handle those questions. So pay attention to what the customer service teams are actually like at a fulfilment house. Try and find a company that has handled your type of product before and so understands the difficulties and challenges of that type of product.

- Scalability – If you grow very suddenly, or have seasonal variations in sales, then you need a company who can handle that. If you sell greetings cards or Christmas decorations then you will get spurts in ordering. Or if you turn out to be very successful and your business grows very quickly, be sure your shipping company has the resources to deal with that efficiently and without fuss.

- Packing – You need to know how your products will be packed. Every shipping company will break something, no matter how robust it is. Also, is it packed in a way that suits your image? If you are selling beautiful soap products do you want them packed in bog-standard bubble wrap or do you want them wrapped in tissue paper?

- Service Level – It's you that the customer will blame if it goes wrong. So make sure you get a commitment to a service level you are happy with.

**Two-Way Street**

Once you have chosen a fulfilment company you may think, 'well that's it, they can do all the work!' But they will have expectations of you too. You aren't just hiring them, you are forming a relationship with them.

What they need from you is the following:
- Inventory – Most of them will warehouse your products for you so they'll need your stock. You can decide how much to give them at any one time and how you will replace that stock

111

once it's gone. Check whether they provide transport to do this or do you have to provide your own.

- Order Information – Automation is the key to an online business. So you need to find a reliable and automated way to get orders to your fulfilment house. Depending on which computer systems they use, you can transfer orders as they come in, or in batches. Some companies will operate the ordering part of the operation as well. If they do, make sure you get all the customer data and orders. You need that customer data to research more details about who your buyers are and who you should be targeting in future.
- Payment – There are different ways that fulfilment houses get paid. You can either build the cost into your orders, then transfer that money every time they fulfil that order, or you can have the company invoice you periodically. If the company is handling the orders it will pay you once it has taken its fee from the transactions.
- Transport – Is your fulfilment house a long way from where your products are? You have to think about the cost of getting the products to the fulfilment house.

---

**TOP TIP**

Always analyse the reports the fulfilment houses give you, it will show you how your products are moving from warehouse to customer. You can keep a close eye on how fast they are shipping orders compared to the dates of the orders.

---

### Database

As your business grows you will find it is more difficult to keep track of orders. So invest in good record keeping software so that you can provide customers with tracking numbers and copies of invoices. It also means you can keep track of what's working and what isn't.

You may find you need more than one database. The things you are likely to want to put in a database are customer information, orders, payments, and product information.

You may need a database that works with your shopping cart,

or you may find it useful to put the information into a spreadsheet in something like Microsoft Excel.

Whatever you choose, it needs to work for you. You need to be able to search it easily. If you need to ask a question like 'How many orders have we had today?' or 'How many customers have viewed the blue widgets?' then you need to be able to find the answers to those questions quickly, and so do your staff if you have any.

# SECTION FIVE

## Marketing and Getting Sales

# Chapter Twenty-Three
## Marketing

So you have set up your website, chosen your products or the services you want to sell, and you're raring to go. But there's a crucial component to being a successful web-preneur, and that is marketing your business.

You have to have a marketing plan and you have to keep working on it. You have to attract customers to your site before they will buy. They won't trip over your shop as they're wandering down the high street, so you have to hook them in. You need a plan, one that involves more than one way to market your business.

If you want to be memorable you have to stand out and there are two ways to do that. You either have such an incredible offer that you're an instant hit, or, and this is more likely, you build layers of what PR people call 'talk-ability'. You want people to talk about you and recommend you.

Imagine a potential customer sees a tweet about you, perhaps something one of their friends has re-tweeted. Will they remember you? They may look at your site if they're interested in your product. Or you may get lost in the avalanche of tweets. But if they then read about you in a magazine, or see you are giving products away in a magazine offer, or they see a newspaper article about you as a new company offering something new, then they are more likely to remember you and take a closer look.

So write a list of every communication channel you can think of that is related to your site. Think about where your customers get their information from. Do they get it from Twitter, from forums, magazines? Is your business going to be driven by word-of-mouth or social media like Facebook? Are they going to see you in the trade papers or the local paper?

All of these channels need content and you can come up with that for free, or pay to advertise.

But how do you get seen? How do you stand out from the crowd? Internet marketing guru Seth Godin is well worth reading on this subject. He says 'Don't taste like chicken!' What does he mean? He means don't be bland and the same as thousands of others. Be different.

He has three D's for formulating a plan:

Distill – Don't waffle. Keep your language sharp, precise, and to the point. It's easier to get your message across in fewer words.

Differentiate – Make your offer as different as you possibly can from the competition. We are bombarded by offers, advertising, and information all day, every day. So make yours stand out.

Discover – Learn about your customers. People buy from people they trust. Simple. If you know your customers, you can talk to them in their language.

## PR

PR makes most business people panic and shut their wallets. They don't understand how it works and they think it's expensive.

But there are lots of things you can do yourself on a shoestring budget.

- List all the events that could be relevant to your business and exploit them. For instance, Christmas, Mother's Day, Bank Holidays, Royal Jubilees, Car Rallies. Anything that you could use to market your products with news or stories.
- Start a database of contacts. Those contacts should be people like journalists, consumer groups, trade organisations, and opinion formers like bloggers. For instance, if you sell make-up, look up beauty bloggers with a large following. And don't leave your list of contacts static, keep it up to date and grow it.
- Work out what your message is in advance, so if a journalist calls you up you are ready with it.
- Network, Network, Network. There is no substitute for this. Get out there and get known.
- Keep a record of everything you have done so that you can follow up on things.
- Monitor the results of your work to see which channels work best for your business then exploit them.

## Chapter Twenty-Four
## Analyse Your Traffic

If you had a bricks-and-mortar shop you could see what your potential customers were interested in by what they stopped to look at or picked up. You could also tell if your products needed more explanation because they would ask you questions.

Online you can't see your customers, but you still need this information so that you can form your marketing plan and re-jig the inventory of the stock you sell.

You need to find out which of your pages and products are popular, how many people are looking at them, and how much time they spend on your pages.

You need to be able to track them from the moment they land on your site, right through to the point where they either leave or press 'Complete Purchase'.

Google Analytics does all of this for you for free.

This will help you test and change every step of the process. It will help you find out whether pay-per-click advertising is working for you, which ads work and which don't, or what organic search results you are getting. It will tell you whether your visitors have visited you before.

### Sign Up

Sign up for a Google Account if you don't have one and go to the Google Analytics website, then click on the 'Access Analytics' button.

If it's your first time accessing the Google Analytics page, you'll probably have to re-enter your Google Account password to begin.

Click on the 'Sign Up' button to create a new account for your website. For an 'Account Name' use your domain name and then enter the time zone you are in.

Google will ask if you want to share your analytics data with other Google products, or third-party services. I would suggest you want to share with other Google products that you will use in your business, like AdWords, AdSense, Webmaster Tools, and so on. Google does give you the option not to share. You have to set up the Tracking Code Configuration. Here, you tell Google Analytics exactly what you want to track. You can tell it whether you are tracking a single domain (yourwebsite.com), a single domain with multiple subdomains (yourwebsite.com, blog.yourwebsite.com, store.yourwebsite.com), or multiple top-level domains (yourwebsite.com, yourwebsite.co.uk, yourwebsite.org).

If you are using Google AdWords for advertising, you link it to Google Analytics by checking the 'AdWords Campaigns' box.

There are advanced features which enable you to track sites built for mobile phones, and to track ad campaigns from other providers.

There is also a 'Custom Setup' tab but if you are just starting out, stick with the Standard configuration until your analytics data needs change.

Once you have done all this you install it onto your website. How you do this will vary on how your site is built. WordPress sites allow you to copy the Google Analytics tracking code into fields specifically designed for tracking scripts from the admin panel. Ask your webmaster about installation.

## Chapter Twenty-Five
## Online Marketing And Advertising

You have to do a number of things to bring people to your site, but however they arrive, it's very important to get the right visitors. Just as with a physical shop, you want hungry buyers and not bored browsers. Once you have those hungry buyers on your site, they're no use to you until they actually buy something.

### Permission Marketing

Getting conversions isn't easy and many internet sites hook in customers by forming a relationship with them, by inviting them to sign up for newsletters or having a forum on the site that they can join. This is known as permission marketing. This means you provide a free service in exchange for their email address and permission to contact them.

If they sign up for your newsletter make sure you give them something that's worth signing up for. If you are selling software then send out newsletters with the latest trends and information. If you do nothing but send out sales letters your subscribers will be rushing to the bottom of the email looking for the 'Unsubscribe' button.

You can contact your subscribers list using a program called an autoresponder, which stores the email addresses of the people who sign up and you can set up newsletters to go out to that list. You can set it up so that they get the email at a certain time of day and the interval between the newsletters. Good autoresponders are www.aweber.com and www.mailchimp.com.

Spend time getting this right, as your relationship with your visitors is crucial. If they get something valuable from you they are more likely to be converted to customers.

# Pay-Per-Click Advertising

There are a few advertising programs on the web but Google AdWords is the biggest. This system can drive highly targeted traffic to your website, i.e. people who are looking to buy exactly what you are selling.

When you search for something on Google you'll notice that there are ads in little boxes down the right hand side of the page, and 'Sponsored Listings' which appear at the top of the page. These are ads purchased by businesses using Google Adwords. It works by letting you pay for a particular search term. So if you've chosen 'Italian hand-made handbags', when someone Googles that term, your ad should come up on that page. If they click on your ad, then you are charged by Google, that's why it's called Pay Per Click. So it allows you to pay each time a user clicks through to your site rather than pay a fixed fee up front. But remember, all it does is get a potential customer to your website – you still have to persuade them to buy from you. Google AdWords creates traffic, not conversions.

How effective the ads are can be measured by the click-through rate, or CTR: the number of people who actually click an ad and end up on your site. You can test, tweak, and monitor the progress of your ads. This is very useful as you can test which ads work and which don't.

In Chapter 2 I talked about making your site friendly for Google using keywords. Well, keywords are the key to AdWords.

## How Does Google AdWords Work?

You have to 'bid' for keywords, and you can set a maximum amount per day or per keyword. The amount you bid on a keyword will have a big effect on how high you appear on the list or search results.

Google also calculates a Quality Score for each of your keywords. This takes into consideration factors like the relevance of your keywords and the text in your ad to the user's search query.

Google also calculates how successful your ads have been to date, so if lots of people click your ad, you will go higher up the list, even if you weren't the highest bidder for a keyword.

Being specific with your keyword is really important because Google monitors relevance. Google has become the most successful search engine because of their ability to match relevance.

Poor keywords are ones that make it difficult for people to find you because they're not relevant. This may be because they are too general. So choose carefully as poor keywords could drive up your costs and your ad may not even show up.

---

TOP TIP

Use Google's keyword tool to help you find a list of good keywords. www.google.com/keywordplanner

Type your main keyword or keyword phrase into the box. This is probably the one you used to create your domain or company name. If not, it is the most obvious keywords for your business. Check the box that asks you to show only results which are closely related to your search terms.

---

Google will show you terms related to your keyword and you'll see what volume that search generates. It also shows you the level of competition and what you will have to pay for those keywords to appear in the top three positions.

This will only be a very rough guide as it doesn't have enough information yet to give you an accurate amount. It doesn't know which domain name it will be linked to or the text in your ad. The estimate you get will be an indicator of the relative cost of your keyword, not the actual cost.

The keyword tool allows you to play around with combinations of categories and words. Take time over this to find words that work for you.

### Exclusions

Bear in mind that there may be combinations of words that you don't want. Lots of people search for things using the word 'free'. You don't want them coming to your site as they're a waste of time; they don't want to buy anything. This really applies to sites selling information or information products. Every time someone clicks through your ad to your site is a cost to you, so you want to exclude these people. You can specify that certain words or combination of words should make your ad show up.

### Bidding for Your Keywords

### Automatic Bidding

If you are new to AdWords you should start off using automatic bidding which allows you to set a daily budget for your campaign. Then AdWords brings you the most clicks possible within that budget. You can even set a Cost Per Click limit, or CPC limit, to make sure the system doesn't bid more than you are willing to spend.

### Manual Bidding

Once you are more familiar with AdWords you can bid manually, this option gives you more control over your account and allows you to set your own price ceiling with maximum CPC bids.

---

**TOP TIP**
When setting your CPC, consider the real value of a click. In other words, how much is a visitor to your website really worth and how likely are they to become a paying customer? You can get conversion statistics by setting up conversion tracking or by using Google Analytics.

---

Bear in mind:
- Higher bids can increase the volume of clicks but can also result in more expensive clicks.
- Lower bids can decrease your volume but also get cheaper clicks.

When you are deciding on your bids you have to consider this trade-off between price and volume.

### Bidding Strategy

To create your bidding strategy you have to consider the following.

- Competition – How many competitors do you have per keyword? Check out how your competitors write their ads. Check their landing pages and read their copy.
- Position – Trying to get into first position is not always the best strategy. It's OK if your ad is third or fourth on the first page as long as you are *on* the first page!
- Budget – Work out how much you want to spend daily and don't bid what you can't afford. But don't go too low either or your ad will only show up to a tiny number of the searches.

## Monitor Your Campaign and the Competition

Monitoring how your campaign is going is crucial. If you run only one campaign with just a few keywords, you can keep an eye on the big players. You'll see the hierarchy changing as some ads disappear and new ones come in. Some ads just seem to stay in forever and this could be a sign that they perform well. You may also notice different ads promoting the same URL. That business is obviously testing what works for them. Notice which ones stay and which ones vanish. The ones that vanish clearly weren't effective.

| TOP TIP |
|---|
| Watch everything! Track these changes and you will learn what works for your business and what doesn't. |

## Chapter Twenty-Six
## Social Media

You probably have a Facebook account, you may tweet, and you may have a LinkedIn profile. So far, so good. And you have probably been told or read various internet gurus telling you that you must be leveraging all these social media platforms to help your business. Well, that's marvellous if you actually know how.

But many new businesses end up with a Facebook page and thousands of 'Likes' that don't get them any sales, a Twitter feed they don't know what to write on so end up talking about their lunch, and a LinkedIn profile full of recommendations that does nothing for them.

People often sign up for these social platforms because of hype and hope. They think that by pumping out marketing messages it will propel their business. It's more complicated than that, and you have to work at it.

Remember, social media is no different from the real world. It's networking, just in a different space. You wouldn't barge into a room full of potential contacts and start broadcasting how great you are. You would check out who was there, who you should talk to, then start a conversation with them, and you would build a relationship over time.

Those relationships would then lead to you getting a reputation, hopefully a good one, and then recommendations. Don't be put off by the fact that you're having to do this online, it is just a different medium for the same behaviour.

Here are my tips for networking success:

- Who Are You Talking To? – You have to know who your potential customers are. Social media is about establishing a reputation and an online identity, which takes time. And you have to know where your customers are. So choose the platform they will use and not the ones you like. It's no good writing updates on your car parts business on LinkedIn if car parts buyers are Twitter users and don't go near LinkedIn. You are more likely to find them on Facebook pages dedicated to petrol-heads. If you are offering bargains then try the forums on www.moneysavingexpert.com because that's where people are looking for a good deal.

- Consider What You Are Saying and Listen – It's not all about shouting your message. Sometimes it's about reading other people's concerns and helping them. Social media is a relationship, not an advertising platform. Add value to conversations online.

- Listen to the Feedback – Pay attention to what other people are saying about you and your business. You can do this by getting automatic updates from Google. Set up a Google alert with www.google.com/alerts. You type in your name or your business name and it will notify you whenever someone is talking about you online. You can also use this to monitor your keywords and what people are saying about those subjects. You can monitor how other brands are doing and industry chatter. This doesn't include Facebook comments as that is guarded by privacy, but tweets and web pages will all flag up. If you want help monitoring Facebook pages and other accounts try www.twentyfeet.com.

- Listen Before you Tweet – Set up a Twitter account and write a good description of yourself and your business and include a photo or a logo. Then listen! You need to start following the competition and the people who are opinion formers in your field. Follow anyone of interest. You can track keywords when they are mentioned using Twitter's search function or using Hootsuite: www.hootsuite.com.

- Connect with People – You will find conversations you want to get involved in, so get involved. Share your thoughts and start a dialogue with people. Engage with people who want to engage with you.

- Provide value – We are all bombarded with rubbish online every day. We want to read stuff that's interesting and that's of value to us. So if you add good or exciting content you will get attention.

- Keep business and personal social media separate. On Facebook, I have multiple pages for my business, including separate pages for Accent Press and Xcite Books, and multiple pages for different book series. I even have one for Million Pound Mum! My personal Facebook, however, I keep separate from all these, as my customers do not necessarily need to know what I had for dinner!

### Which Social Media Should I Use?

There are lots of social media channels that offer their users different experiences. The less-used ones are www.foursquare.com, www.flickr.com and www.YouTube.com which may all be useful for your business. Google+ is also gaining in popularity.

The Big Three are:

Facebook – www.facebook.com

Twitter

LinkedIn

These are the three platforms that most people are familiar with. People use them differently and experience them differently. Facebook is like a giant online club with lots of smaller clubs inside it. Anyone can join in but what you say will only be available to your sub-club.

Twitter is ephemeral and less personal. When you tweet – which means putting a posting up, like updating your Facebook status – you can only use 140 characters. That's characters, not letters, so you have to count the spaces. It forces you to be really precise. People often access it through a third-party application like TweetDeck – www.tweetdeck.com – or mobile apps.

LinkedIn has been described as a 'Facebook for Suits'. It's a network for professionals and is more about connecting with other people than talking about your life.

I am going to focus on Facebook and Twitter as these are the ones most used for marketing.

## Marketing with Facebook

Facebook allows you to have a page for your business. If you are a Facebook user, I am sure that many businesses have sent you a 'Please Like My Page' link. It's very easy to set up, so it's worth doing. If someone comments on your page, that comment, hopefully a testimonial, will be seen by all their friends. If their friends then take a look and also write a comment, then all their friends see it, and so on. As I mentioned earlier, we love Facebook pages at Accent Press, and I make them for as many of our series as possible. These are very helpful because not only can we let people know about new publications, we can also target them to niche groups who may have interests in the themes of a particular series.

You may have noticed ads that appear down the right hand side of the page. These are targeted to what Facebook thinks you will want. Carefully targeted Facebook ads can be very beneficial for a variety of reasons. You can target them to interested parties to maximise their chance of success. You can even target them via nationality, which is very useful for us because some books do better in certain countries than others.

---

**TOP TIP**

You should think of it as setting up a fan club for your business, rather than somewhere to sell stuff.

---

## Setting up a Page

One of Facebook's big pluses is that it's easy to use, and setting up a page is pretty simple. To make it interesting for your business, you can add things to it like a feed from your blog if you have one. You do this through the 'Notes' application and it displays each blog entry as an update which appears in all your fans' 'news feeds'. This means that your Facebook page will have regularly updated content, if you are updating your blog, that is. If your blog sits idle from one month to the next then nothing will update!

## Marketing with Twitter

Twitter is one big community rather than a collection of smaller ones that intersect. So it's much harder to build a community on Twitter than Facebook. But the benefit is you can access everything that is being said about you on the feed in one go.

Twitter can be a very effective way to promote yourself and your business, but you have to get a following first. Be careful of just using it for advertising. Think of how you would feel if someone you were following just started advertising and didn't tweet anything you were interested in. You would 'unfollow' them pretty quickly, wouldn't you?

Look for Your Customers

You can find tweets about your products or about the marketplace you operate in. People often use Twitter to moan, so you can see what sort of language they are using and what they don't want. Once you know what they *don't* want, you can get a better idea of what they *do* want.

Once you have found someone who is looking for something you sell, you can interact with them and then sell to them. Please note I said interact first!

How to Get a Following

What you want is a large number of relevant followers, people who may actually buy from you or recommend you. We humans are herd animals; we like to follow the crowd, so the more followers you have the more people will think you're worth following.

The key is to build momentum. Too many people start tweeting and then give up.

- You have to tweet, tweet, and tweet again.
- You must tweet content that is interesting to your audience.
- Don't be afraid to be controversial because that starts conversations.
- It doesn't matter if you have no followers to start with, keep tweeting!

### Look for People to Follow

There are some people who follow no one and just tweet to their followers. But the smart thing to do is to follow relevant people. Search Twitter for keywords that relate to you and your market.

- Find the most interesting people and check their profiles.
- Do they tweet often and do they have a lot of followers?
- Look at who they follow and who follows them.
- Don't follow anyone who has written only handful of tweets
- Follow relevant people.
- Start with up to 100 people. If you follow thousands, you can't keep track of them all. So target who you follow carefully.

If you pick the right people, a lot of them will follow you back. The key is to be active on Twitter. You can organise your Twitter using www.TweetDeck.com or www.HootSuite.com. You can set up lists of the people you follow to make it easier.

---

**BEWARE!**
There are companies who will get you lots of followers for a price. But what kind of followers? It's no use to you having an army of uninterested followers. They won't be targeted and the companies may have broken the Twitter terms and conditions to get them. So you could end up with a suspended account.

---

# SECTION SIX

## Protecting Your Customers

## Chapter Twenty-Seven
## Policies You Must Have

When you shop online you expect certain standards. You want to know that the business you are buying from respects your privacy and your security, so you need to put these things in place for your business.

Your customers are your life. Without them, you have no business, so making sure they feel loved and cared for is very important. Think of some very successful businesses and you will find that they have a reputation, or at least a marketing message, that says they think about their customers.

If you don't think about your customers' experience of you, you will come to regret it. You have been researching and planning what you are going to sell, how you are going to sell it, and who you are going to sell it to. Now you need to spend time on making sure you are taking care of your customers.

### Promises, Promises

Telling a customer what they can expect of you is a good way to win their trust. It also adds value. If you are competing with ten other companies, how are you going to get people to buy from you? Make them feel they can trust you.

Whatever it is you can promise your customer, write it out and put it on your website.

Tell them:

- How they can contact you and when. If you have a phone line, is it manned 9-5, five days a week?
- How quickly you will respond to any of their queries.
- What is special about your offer to them. Make them feel you are talking directly to them. Are you offering a huge range, or do you scour the globe looking for the best products for them? Do you constantly look at prices elsewhere to make sure you are getting bargains for them?

- If you welcome feedback and provide a form or an email address for them to contact you.

You can add anything you like to your promise as long as you are sure you can live up to it. Don't tie yourself to a promise you can't keep.

## Privacy

No one likes to think that their details are floating around the internet for anyone to see. So you must have a privacy policy.

You must tell your customer:

- Details of what information about them you collect.
- How you collect, store, and use that information.
- If you share the information with anyone, you must tell the customer.
- You must give instructions on how customers can change or remove their information from your site.
- Tell them if you use cookies. When you visit a website, a cookie is a small piece of data sent from that website and stored in your web browser. When you visit the site again, the data stored in the cookie is sent back to the website by the browser to tell them about your previous activity.
- You should clearly state that you have a commitment to keeping their data private and secure.

### Terms and Conditions – User Agreements

These are agreements between you and your visitors and customers. It sets out the conditions for using your site. You can either put a static page on your site, or you may find that the nature of your business means you want your customers to accept your T&Cs before they can use your site. They do this through pressing an 'Accept' button on a T&C's pop-up page. If you have ever used iTunes or similar websites you will be familiar with this. Once the T&C's are accepted, this is legally binding.

What you should include:

- How customers can or can't use your site – This may include things like adding abusive comments on review pages or on a forum.

- Who is allowed to visit – There may be restrictions on who goes to your site. If you are an online wine merchant, you might want to spell out that your customers need to be of legal age to buy alcohol.
- Liabilities – If there are any legal disputes you have to provide information over where disputes will be settled, so if you are in the UK, will they be settled in the UK?
- Any other policies – You will want to point out the details of other policies such as shipping, returns, refunds, and complaints.

Let's look at the other policies in detail.

### Returns Policy

- You must tell customers how, when, and for what reasons they are allowed to return products. You don't want them to get a shock when they thought they could return something and they can't.
- Conditions of Use – Tell them when they are allowed and when they are not allowed to return a product. For instance, if you sell cosmetics, are they allowed to return them if they've tried them, or must the products come back unopened?
- Return Postage and Packing – Will you pay to get the product back, or must they foot the bill for the postage?
- Time – Set a maximum number of days for returning an item.
- Exceptions – If there are items that can't be returned, explain what they are. For instance, you may not want to accept sale items in returns.
- Refunds – State clearly whether they get their money back or whether they get a credit note they can use on your site.
- Third Parties – This applies if you sell items from third party vendors. You must be able to direct your customers to their returns policy. They will probably have a returns policy that would supersede anything you have on your site.

### Children

If you are selling to children or offering services to them, such as online games, then you have to reassure their parents that their children are safe. Get parental consent before collecting information and allow parents to see all that information and change or delete it.

## Forums and Chat rooms

You will need to make your guidelines clear to anyone who wants to use these.

- You should set out who can join and how they register.
- You also need to tell them who is monitoring the chat and what material is appropriate, and when you'll remove it if it is inappropriate.

## Social Media

Just because you are asking your customers to have a relationship with you on an external site doesn't mean you absolve yourself of all responsibility there.

- You should treat these extra spaces as an extension of your business.
- You must tell customers what will happen to their information if you collect it from these sites.

## Third parties

- If you sell products from other sites or you have links to other sites that you don't own, then tell your customers.
- Show how you use these links and whether you endorse the information on there.

## Look after your Customer

At the end of the day, all of these policies are there to make sure that your relationship with your customer is conducted with mutual understanding of both your responsibilities.

Of course, things will always go wrong, so when they do, apologise as fast as possible and correct the problem quickly. Customers will often forgive your mistake if you show you care.

So email them immediately or call them if you have stated in your policy that you may call their landline or mobile to resolve a difficulty. And offer a refund or give them a gift. Whatever you decide to do, you must make the customer feel loved, appreciated, and above all, valued.

# Chapter Twenty-Eight
## Security

Have you ever had your emails hacked? Worrying and annoying, isn't it? Do you worry that if you shop at an online store that your credit card details may not be safe?

Well, it's not just customers who can fall victim to cyber-crime, it's the shops too. It's also your responsibility to protect your customer from fraud or identity theft.

You can minimise the risk by keeping a close eye on credit card payments and keeping your customers' data as secure as possible.

### Information

You have to protect customer information. Customers want to know what you will collect from them, what you'll do with it, and how safe you will keep it.

It's a good idea to get and display an SSL certificate. These are a vital piece of technology for anyone running an online business as they help protect transactions and customer information.

SSL stands for 'Secure Sockets Layer' and is a data encryption protocol, which basically means that it will scramble any data as it travels across the net. So it's a bit like travelling in a blacked-out car rather than a glass carriage. It protects your information during payment transactions. This means it turns your information into a code that can only be read by a third party who has the key to read the information, so it can't be stolen easily.

This means your customers can verify that you are who you say you are, making your website or your online business much more trustworthy. You may have seen a padlock sign on some sites, or the URL bar may turn green. This shows there is an SSL Certificate.

## Getting an SSL

You can either get it from an approved vendor like www.VeriSign.co.uk or from your web host or domain registration company.

There are different levels of SSL and the higher the encryption rate the more expensive they are. A higher encryption rate makes them more difficult to hack. The industry standard is 128 bit encryption.

If you are not sure you need it then you can get a 30-day free trial from VeriSign.

## Showing Your Credentials

If there are any badges of approval you can show on your site then put them up. Anything that shows you are a legitimate business is a good idea. For instance, if you are a travel agent, display your ATOL membership somewhere prominent on your pages. Customers have a bewildering array of choice, so as well as adding value to your proposition, add trust, and your customers will come back to you time and time again.

## Risk Analysis

If you were trying to make your house more secure you would probably walk around the house looking to see where you are vulnerable. Do those windows have locks? Am I leaving my iPad lying around where people can see it through the window?

The same goes for your business. You need to do a security analysis. So make a list of the potential threats to your business.

- Internal Threats – You may not want to think that anything could go wrong from inside your company, but it can, either deliberately or accidentally. You could end up being the victim of a malicious act. Make sure you trust your staff and you still only give them access to things you can trust them with. But accidental errors can cause havoc. So look around your business and think 'If it can go wrong, it will go wrong!' and plan accordingly.
- Failures – What if your computers crash or your network goes

down? Can you cope? If your internet crashes, how long will it take your internet provider to get it up and running again? If you have to wait three days, that's three days of sales you are losing, and you may never get those customers back as they won't visit again.

**Simple Preventative Measures**

There are things you can do to minimise the risk of things going wrong. If you have worked for a large company you will probably have been irritated by the things you had to do to stay secure, such as regularly changing your password. But now you are on the other side of the fence you will realise that these things are important.

- Change your password regularly and make your staff do the same.
- Back up data regularly. You should schedule this, not just do it when you remember. Though if you have just completed something critical, back it up straight away.
- Get software updates regularly. It's a good idea to turn on the 'Automatic Update' feature.
- If you have servers or computers that are critical to your business, secure them.
- Maintain active antivirus software and firewalls on your computers and servers.
- Have physical protection like fire, smoke, and burglar alarms.
- If you store paper copies of data, keep them in locked filing cabinets.
- Use a Virtual Private Network, or VPN, when sending information over a wireless connection. This creates a protective wall around your connection and keeps out anyone who hasn't been granted access. You can buy a wireless VPN firewall from companies like www.Netgear.com or www.Belkin.com. If you are planning on spending a lot of time in those cafés drinking lattes while you work then you can sign up for a subscription VPN service.
- Keep food and drink away from any systems that are critical.

**TOP TIP**

It's a good idea to store all your data off-site on another server or in cloud storage. Cloud storage means backing up your data to the internet on a secure site, there's lesser risk of losing your data and you can access it from anywhere by going online and logging in to your account at that site. Try cloud facilities like Google Drive or Dropbox. Some services are free and some charge a monthly fee for storing large amounts of data.

So if your building burns down you can still run your business from somewhere else. Or if you want to spend a month in Marbella, you might be able to run it from your laptop on the beach while the kids are paddling!

## Wireless World

We live in an increasingly wireless world, doing business on tablet computer while out and about. But that leaves us open to threats so it's important whether you are in or out of the office to stay secure. If you think that hackers are only interested in big business then you'd be wrong. Many small businesses are easier to hack because their owners don't take precautions.

What you have to remember when you use wireless computing is that you are sharing a signal that is being broadcast to all around you. Determined hackers have a depressingly large arsenal of tools to get in. No security system will give you 100% protection, but you can do things to keep yourself more secure and most of them are common sense.

- Shut Down – When you aren't using your computer, shut it down, especially overnight.
- Firewalls – A firewall on your computer gives you a layer of protection.
- Make sure your wireless is secured with the Wi-Fi Protected Access setting, or WPA. Make sure all your devices are configured to use this. If not, your computer will revert to the default setting which is Wired Equivalent Privacy or WEP.

This offers less protection than WPA.

- Don't Go Looking – Turn off the broadcast feature that automatically goes looking for a network to join. Manually enter your login information or the name of the network you want to join.
- Don't Over-share – Limit who shares what in your business. If you have networked computers, limit which files or directories people have access to.

### Two-Factor Authentication

If you use Gmail you may have noticed you can have two authentications, you enter your password then Google sends you a text message with a number code which you enter on the site. To set this up go to your Google account and go to the Account Settings. You'll find Using 2-Step Verification in the Personal Settings for Security.

---

**TOP TIP**
Nothing can keep you 100% safe, but if you use a combination of the right software and common sense rules you stand a better chance of not being hacked or becoming the victim of fraud.

---

## And Finally ...

You may use the internet every day but are slightly daunted by having to tame it to start a business. But it doesn't have to be a huge undertaking, and you don't have to learn it all at once. You can start small. Dip your toe in the water by selling on eBay or Amazon to see how you get on. There is a worldwide audience for whatever it is you want to sell, and you can get to it from your laptop. It can be done, slowly and surely – anyone who can learn to run a business can learn to run one online.

You don't need buckets of capital or a string of degrees, just a willingness to learn. I did it! So if you are passionate about wanting to run your own life, then your future may be online.

Good Luck!

# Useful Resources

**Domain Names**
www.123-reg.co.uk

**Affiliate Networks**
www.affiliatewindow.com
www.cj.com

**Online Marketplaces**
www.amazon.co.uk
www.ebay.co.uk

**Hosted e-Commerce**
www.bigcommerce.com

**Freelance Networks**
www.fiverr.com
www.elance.com
www.peopleperhour.com

**Blogging Software**
www.blogger.com
www.wordpress.com

**Online Payment Systems**
www.paypal.com
www.worldpay.com

**Internet Industry Research**
www.mintel.com
www.forester.co.uk

**Social Media**
www.facebook.com
www.twitter.com
www.linkedin.com
www.foursquare.com

www.flickr.com
www.youtube.com

## Business Advice & Networks
www.businesslink.gov.uk
www.britishchambers.org.uk
www.fsb.org.uk

# How To Be A Million Pound Mum
## Hazel Cushion

For more information about **Hazel Cushion**
and other **Accent Press** titles
please visit

www.accentpress.co.uk

Lightning Source UK Ltd.
Milton Keynes UK
UKOW04f2358260515

252343UK00001B/20/P